I0813929

LOS ANGELES
Like a Local

LOS ANGELES Like a Local

BY THE PEOPLE WHO CALL IT HOME

Contents

meet the locals

SARAH BENNETT

Sarah's family has lived in the L.A. area for generations. As an educator and journalist, Sarah loves sharing the stories of the land that raised her. Her mom, a former MGM Studios executive assistant, would be proud.

RYAN GAJEWSKI

Lifelong L.A. resident Ryan is a staff editor at The Hollywood Reporter. *When he's not writing, he's sniffing out banh mi, watching comedy, and exploring movie studio lots.*

ANITA LITTLE

Writer and editor Anita has been in L.A. for over a decade, and currently lives in Culver City with her boyfriend and cat. She unwinds by wandering the stacks in indie bookstores and hiking scenic beach trails.

EVA RECINOS

Born and raised in Los Angeles, Eva is an arts and culture writer. You'll spot her scribbling away in cafés or wandering around the city's museums. She hasn't owned a car in years so, yes, people do walk in L.A.

Los Angeles

WELCOME TO THE CITY

Los Angeles – it's all movie star glamour and edgy hip-hop beats, right? Well, yes and no. Much of what you've likely imagined about the city is true: the palm-tree-lined streets, the celebrity sightings, the looming letters of the Hollywood sign. Angelenos really do spend a lot of time outside (who wouldn't when the weather's this good) and the presence of the entertainment industry is basically inescapable. But that doesn't even begin to capture what the real L.A. is like. This isn't just some glossy playground for the rich and famous – it's a sprawling city that millions of ordinary people call home.

And it's those folk who give L.A. its heart. They're out-there thinkers launching buzzing pop-ups, fresh-faced hopefuls following artistic dreams, and immigrants adding new flavors to the epic local food scene. Angelenos may be known for their sunny outlook, though that's not to say that life's always easy. Wildfires have devastated vast areas of the city, forcing people from their homes and destroying numerous nature reserves. Locals also hustle hard to afford the cost of living, and the creep of gentrification is as ever present as the traffic (seriously, whole years are lost stuck in cars). But Angelenos have forged strong communities across the freeways and are fiercely determined to keep L.A. a city for all.

And that's where this book takes you. Beyond the Walk of Fame and into neighborhoods covered with historic street art. To quirky mom-and-pop shops hiding in strip malls and late-night taquerias serving the best birria outside of Mexico. Because that's where the real L.A. lies – in the everyday moments and interactions. So forget everything you've seen on screen, and let us show you the city through the eyes of the locals.

Liked by the locals

"I love that L.A. is so sprawling and diverse that it can't possibly be known in one visit – or even one lifetime. Just when you think you've seen it all, you discover a new pocket to explore, or stumble upon an emerging culture to dive into."

SARAH BENNETT,
FOOD AND CULTURE JOURNALIST

The sun shines on L.A. for around 300 days a year, but the city still has distinct seasons, each with its own traditions and events.

Los Angeles

THROUGH THE YEAR

SPRING

FESTIVAL FUN

Despite a mild winter, Angelenos still celebrate the arrival of spring with a range of festivals across the city. The party continues throughout the season, with St. Patrick's Day in March and Cinco de Mayo in May.

TRAIL TIME

As the days get warmer, L.A.'s super-healthy residents don their best workout gear, lace up their sneakers, and hit the mountain trails to clear the cobwebs.

SHOP 'TIL YOU DROP

The change of season, however minimal, calls for a change of clothes and interior decor. Style mavens head to the likes of the Rose Bowl Flea Market, the Melrose Trading Post, and the Long Beach Antique Market to purge and replenish their wardrobes and homes.

SUMMER

TEAM PLAYER

For many Angelenos, summer revolves around baseball games. Clad head to toe in blue, locals flock to Dodger Stadium each weekend to cheer on their team. Go Dodgers!

ALFRESCO MUSIC

Bands and fans move outside to take advantage of the weather at venues like the Greek Theatre, Hollywood Bowl, Levitt Pavilion, and Hollywood Forever Cemetery (yes, you read that right).

PRIDE PARADE

Rainbow flags fly on the second weekend in June, when L.A.'s out-and-proud residents and their allies take to the streets to celebrate the community.

WHERE'S THE SUN?

L.A. doesn't play by the rules and neither does its weather. Summer often sees cloudy, overcast skies, earning the months the nicknames "Gray May," "June Gloom," "No-Sky July," and "Fogust."

FALL

SPOOKY SEASON

The costumes, the makeup, the movies: Hollywood and Halloween have a lot in common. So it's not really surprising that Angelenos throw themselves into the holiday, checking out the theme parks' haunted houses, the Los Angeles Haunted Hayride, and Queen Mary's Dark Harbor.

DÍA DE LOS MUERTOS

On the Day of the Dead, seemingly everyone, from first-generation Mexican immigrants to East Coast transplants, paints their face, dons floral crowns, and parties into the night.

APPLE EVERYTHING

Come fall, locals have one thing on their mind: apples. On the weekends, they drive out to nearby orchards to take advantage of the harvest, sipping fresh cider, and munching on comforting pies. Who said L.A. couldn't be cozy?

WINTER

HOLIDAY CHEER

Okay, you're never going to get a white Christmas in L.A., but in this city you have to fake it till you make it. Locals ice-skate in palm tree-lined Pershing Square and cover their homes in fake snow, bright lights, and blow-up Santas.

NEW YEAR PARADES

It wouldn't be a holiday without a parade. Angelenos ring in the New Year at Pasadena's flower-filled Tournament of Roses Parade and Chinatown's Golden Dragon Parade.

RAINY DAYS

Due to their rarity, a rainy day is a big event in L.A. Expect social media to blow up at the first droplet of water, and the freeways to grind to a complete and utter halt.

There's an art to being an Angeleno, from the do's and don'ts of eating out to negotiating the city's sprawling streets. Here's a breakdown of all you need to know.

Los Angeles

KNOW-HOW

For a directory of health and safety resources, safe spaces, and accessibility information, turn to page 186. For everything else, read on.

EAT

Los Angeles is a city of foodies, so it makes sense that – whatever the hour – there's always some place serving up something truly delicious. Brunch is a huge deal on weekends, with Angelenos waiting in line from 10a.m. for an artful stack of pancakes and a breakfast mimosa. As for dinner, reservations are recommended wherever possible, though some restaurants do have space at the bar for walk-ins.

DRINK

Since L.A. temperatures are pretty mild, the city has plenty of patio cafés and rooftop bars where locals gather for a drink, safe in the knowledge that the sun will (pretty much) always be shining. A beer mostly goes for less than $10, a glass of wine is around $12, and a craft cocktail can cost an eye-watering $20. Thankfully, happy hours are common and make things more affordable. Most bars close around 2a.m.

SHOP

Angelenos love crafting their own unique styles, so it's no surprise they generally prefer to shop at indie boutiques, vintage stores, and flea markets over malls and chain stores. Stores tend to open between 9 and 10a.m., with most closing around 5 or 6p.m. (though malls typically stay open until around 9p.m.). Tip: wherever you're parting with your paycheck, be sure to bring a tote bag. You'll save yourself a potential charge for a plastic one, and you're doing your part for the environment.

ARTS & CULTURE

Culture usually comes at a price in L.A., with entry to museums and galleries costing anywhere from $9 at smaller venues to $25 for larger institutions. Some also require reservations (even if they are free) so always check ahead. Likewise, it's sensible to book movie tickets before rocking up at the theater.

NIGHTLIFE

Rush hour traffic (think of the opening scene of *La La Land*) makes it pretty difficult to have a spontaneous drink during the week, so Angelenos instead go big on weekends. Predrinking takes place at home or during happy hour. Clubs get going around 10p.m. and generally close at 2a.m. As for what to wear, it depends on the venue: casual clothing is A-OK for a dive bar, while swankier clubs require fancier attire. No matter the place, be sure to carry ID, have a designated driver, and cash for parking.

OUTDOORS

Reading a book on the beach is one of life's simple pleasures, as is chatting with pals over a teetotal picnic (alcohol is prohibited in the city's parks). But there's a lot of dry brush in Los Angeles and wildfires do happen, so be sensible and follow any signs about fire safety. And be sure to take your trash with you – littering carries a fine in California.

Keep in mind

Here are some more tips and tidbits that will help you fit in like a local.

» **Contactless** Most places take cards and methods like Apple Pay, but bring some cash for things like parking.

» **No smoking** Lighting up in public parks, beaches, bus stops, farmers' markets, and outdoor eating areas is banned.

» **Tipping** Adding at least 15, if not 20, percent to your bill is a must at restaurants, bars, and even food trucks.

» **Stay hydrated** Plenty of cafés and restaurants are happy to refill your reusable water bottle – just ask nicely.

GETTING AROUND

Understanding the setup of Los Angeles takes some patience. Sitting within Los Angeles County, with the Pacific Ocean to the west and San Francisco to the north, L.A. comprises various neighborhoods (or communities) and cities (88 of them, to be specific). Chinatown and Bel Air are neighborhoods, for example, while Beverly Hills and Pasadena are technically cities. Angelenos live all over, but most visitors tend to concentrate on the roughly central section between Downtown and Santa Monica. When it comes to navigating the city, locals orient themselves around freeways. The 10 travels east to west, the 110 goes north to south, and the 405 traces the city's western edge.

Once you've got your bearings, L.A. is pretty easy to navigate. But to help you along, we've provided what3words addresses for each sight in this book, meaning you can quickly pinpoint exactly where you're heading.

On foot

It's a myth that locals don't walk in Los Angeles. The city sprawls, yes, and most people own cars (not everyone, mind), but many prefer to enjoy the city's mild climate and palm tree-lined streets by walking. A few words of advice before you set off: distances aren't short (Downtown to Santa Monica is around 15 miles/24 km), and not all neighborhoods are pedestrian friendly (we're looking at you, Bel Air). So you're best off focusing on an area at a time, rather than trying to cover the whole city in one go – Downtown, Santa Monica, the Hollywoods, and Venice are all good places to start. And remember: wear sunscreen, as some blocks don't offer much shade.

On wheels

Biking is not for the faint of heart here in car-happy L.A., but if you're willing to brave it, there are some dedicated bike lanes around the city. Just be sure to put on a helmet before zooming off.

The most relaxed bike paths are on the oceanfront, between Santa Monica and Redondo, and you'll find plenty of bike rentals nearby. If you're exploring more urban areas, Metro Bike Share has docking stations across the city. Just purchase a pass online, download the app, and get pedaling on a classic or electric bike. A 30-minute ride costs $1.75, or you can purchase a $5 one-day pass, which gives you an unlimited number of rides under 30 minutes (though usual charges apply after that). ***https://bikeshare.metro.net***

By public transportation

Angelenos like to complain about the Metro, but, in fact, it's a perfectly good way of getting around. Trains run north to south across the city, and also east to west; buses go pretty much everywhere. It's worth buying a $2 TAP card and loading it up with money (it's $1.75 for a one-way fare).

The Los Angeles Department of Transportation's DASH bus service also covers select areas of the city, including downtown L.A., though it doesn't cover as much ground as the Metro.

By car or taxi

Most Angelenos own a car and famously spend a chunk of their lives at the wheel. If you're looking to join them on the road, search for deals on Kayak or Getaround. Use your blinkers and always check your blind spot (though don't assume everyone else will do the same). Parking can be a nightmare so always do your research – including if your destination has a dedicated parking lot, meters, or, well, no parking at all. And be aware that some parking meters take only credit cards or coins.

Prefer to be driven rather than drive? Uber and Lyft are both popular in L.A. though prices can get high, particularly when the city is hosting events.

Download these

We recommend you download these apps to help you get about the city.

WHAT3WORDS

Your geocoding friend

A what3words address is a simple way to communicate any precise location on earth, using just three random words. ///lime.liner.organs, for example, is the code for the entrance to the Griffith Observatory. Simply download the free what3words app, type a what3words address into the search bar, and you'll know exactly where to go.

TRANSIT

Your local transportation service

Map out your journey ahead with Transit, the official Metro app. Not only will it tell you when to transfer to different lines, and which parts of the trip you'll have to walk, but it estimates times when the next bus or train will arrive. No sweat.

L.A. is a sprawling city of cities, and every neighborhood has its own distinct vibe. Here, we take a look at some of our favorites.

Los Angeles
NEIGHBORHOODS

Beverly Hills
90210: it's L.A.'s – heck, the world's – most well-known zip code. And it has all the fancy estates, manicured lawns, and designer boutiques you'd expect from such an iconic haunt of the rich and famous. *{map 3}*

Boyle Heights/East L.A.
This historic area east of Downtown is home to a mostly Mexican community, whose heritage shines through in the robust street food culture and vibrant murals. *{map 1}*

Culver City
The heart of the movie industry in the 1920s, Culver City is now a tech boomtown. It's popular with young professionals, who love its rad mix of dining and culture, and the friendly, small-town feel. *{map 4}*

Downtown
Decades of redevelopment cash have seen the once-seedy Downtown go upscale. These days, there's barely a block without a trendy new shopping district, art gallery, or restaurant, or a group of revelers hitting up the buzzing nightlife scene. *{map 1}*

Echo Park
Anchored by its namesake park and lake, this gentrified Latinx area is hipster central. In L.A., that means music venues, chic boutiques, and lots of late-night taco trucks. *{map 1}*

Fairfax
When Angelenos don't have weekend plans, they come to this central patch for the Farmers' Market and The Grove. The rest of the time, it's a hub for the city's Jewish community, with popular delis attracting lines throughout the day. *{map 3}*

Hollywood
Famed for its unique mix of glitz and grit, plus some pretty iconic landmarks, Hollywood is – of course – the L.A. you know and love from the movies. Expect cinema history and snap-happy tourists aplenty. *{map 3}*

Inglewood

Now home to the biggest and priciest football stadium ever built, not to mention a shiny new NBA arena, this historically Black community is undergoing rapid change as it becomes the latest hub for tourism and sports entertainment. *{map 4}*

Koreatown

A large Korean population has lived in this neighborhood since the 1960s, though they've been joined in more recent years by other L.A. newcomers. And who can blame them? With cheap rent, convenient shops, and abundant dining, Koreatown has a lot going for it. *{map 2}*

Little Tokyo

Fun fact: Little Tokyo is one of only three official Japantowns remaining in the U.S. It's a lively hub of Japanese American history and culture, crammed with cool stores and ever-busy food joints. *{map 1}*

Long Beach

Once the most diverse large city in the U.S., this coastal port is a laid-back mix of urban and suburban. Here, you'll find everyone from college kids to stay-at-home parents to punkers all drinking at the same coffee shops and bars. *{map 5}*

Los Feliz

With its Old Hollywood bungalows and scenic hillside setting, it's not hard to see why well-heeled creatives are drawn to this artsy enclave. Welcoming, walkable, and packed with trendy cafés and posh galleries, it oozes a vibe that's seriously cool. *{map 2}*

Pasadena

This has long been the suburb of choice for those wanting to escape the L.A. hubbub and raise a family. Its Old Town gently bustles with parents and retired residents, all browsing the long stretch of chain and independent stores. *{map 6}*

Santa Monica

This neighborhood may be luxe, but it's never loud about it. Instead, it's a center of easygoing beach vibes, with a daily cast of locals (and a steady stream of tourists) enjoying the sunsets, ocean breezes, and beautiful hikes. *{map 4}*

Venice

Home to an eclectic mix of tech bros, tourists, and a slowly disappearing immigrant community, this still-funky beach town is famous for its postcard-ready canals and anything-goes boardwalk. Parking is always a battle, but locals love it anyway. *{map 4}*

West Hollywood

Affectionately known as WeHo to the young creatives who live here, this area has long been the place to come for a good time. Formerly a gambling haven in the 1920s, it's now home to a thumping nightlife scene and a lively LGBTQ+ community. *{map 3}*

Los Angeles

ON THE MAP

Whether you're looking for your new favorite spot or want to check out what each part of Los Angeles has to offer, our maps – along with handy map references throughout the book – have you covered.

PALMDALE
CA-14
I-5
CA-14
Angeles National Forest
SANTA CLARITA
6
SAN FERNANDO
Santa Gabriel Mountains
NORTHRIDGE
SUN VALLEY
Verdugo Mountains
I-210
CALABASAS
VAN NUYS
BURBANK
ALTADENA
2
GLENDALE
PASADENA
I-210
GLENDORA
3
SAN GABRIEL
EL MONTE
COVINA
TOPANGA
HOLLY-WOOD
1
I-10
4
DOWNTOWN
MONTEREY PARK
CA-1
I-10
SANTA MONICA
CULVER CITY
5
CA-60
WALNUT
VENICE
DOWNEY
SOUTHGATE
INGLEWOOD
WATTS
LA HABRA
HAWTHORNE
COMPTON
PARAMOUNT
FULLERTON
Santa Monica Bay
REDONDO BEACH
ANAHEIM
CARSON
TORRANCE
SIGNAL HILL
I-5
GARDEN GROVE
LONG BEACH
PALOS VERDES
NAPLES
SANTA ANA
SAN PEDRO
I-405
HUNTINGTON BEACH
COSTA MESA
CA-1
San Pedro Bay

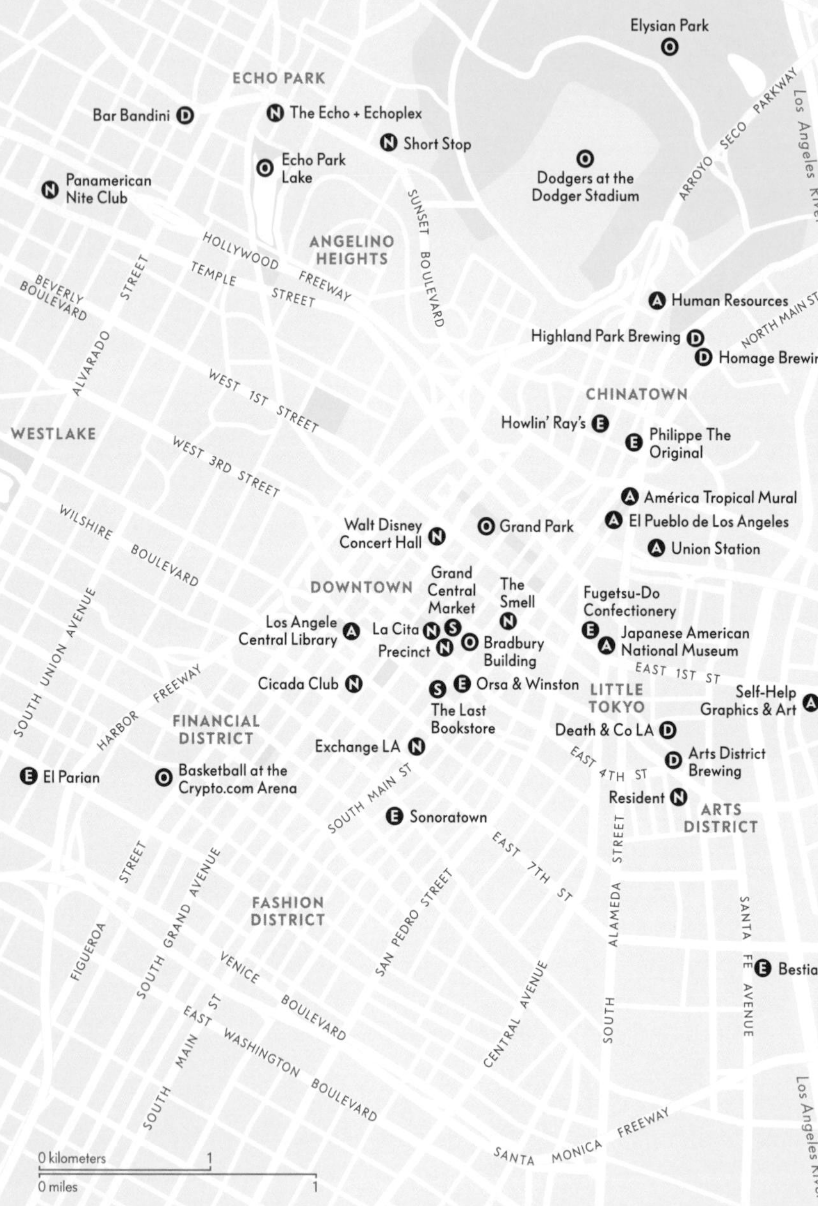

Elysian Park
ECHO PARK
Bar Bandini
The Echo + Echoplex
Short Stop
Echo Park Lake
Dodgers at the Dodger Stadium
Panamerican Nite Club
ARROYO SECO PARKWAY
Los Angeles River
SUNSET BOULEVARD
HOLLYWOOD FREEWAY
ANGELINO HEIGHTS
TEMPLE STREET
BEVERLY BOULEVARD
STREET
ALVARADO
Human Resources
NORTH MAIN ST
Highland Park Brewing
Homage Brewing
WEST 1ST STREET
CHINATOWN
Howlin' Ray's
Philippe The Original
WESTLAKE
WEST 3RD STREET
América Tropical Mural
El Pueblo de Los Angeles
Union Station
WILSHIRE BOULEVARD
Walt Disney Concert Hall
Grand Park
DOWNTOWN
Grand Central Market
The Smell
Fugetsu-Do Confectionery
Los Angele Central Library
La Cita
Precinct
Bradbury Building
Japanese American National Museum
EAST 1ST ST
SOUTH UNION AVENUE
HARBOR FREEWAY
Cicada Club
Orsa & Winston
The Last Bookstore
LITTLE TOKYO
Self-Help Graphics & Art
FINANCIAL DISTRICT
Exchange LA
Death & Co LA
EAST 4TH ST
Arts District Brewing
El Parian
Basketball at the Crypto.com Arena
SOUTH MAIN ST
Resident
ARTS DISTRICT
Sonoratown
EAST 7TH ST
STREET
SOUTH GRAND AVENUE
FIGUEROA
FASHION DISTRICT
SAN PEDRO STREET
ALAMEDA STREET
SOUTH
SANTA FE AVENUE
Bestia
VENICE BOULEVARD
CENTRAL AVENUE
EAST WASHINGTON BOULEVARD
SOUTH MAIN ST
SANTA MONICA FREEWAY
0 kilometers 1
0 miles 1

LINCOLN HEIGHTS

1

GOLDEN STATE FREEWAY

Re/Arte Centro Literario
S
A Mariachi Plaza

BOYLE HEIGHTS

SANTA ANA

E EAT

D DRINK

S SHOP

A ARTS & CULTURE

N NIGHTLIFE

O OUTDOORS

0 kilometers 1
0 miles 1
VENTURA FREEWAY
GLENDALE
NORTH GLENDALE AVE
NORTH VERDUGO ROAD
Electric Dusk Drive-In
WEST BROADWAY
Museum of Neon Art
WEST COLORADO ST
SAN FERNANDO ROAD
Los Angeles Zoo
Los Angeles River
CRYSTAL SPRINGS DRIVE
Griffith Park
Hollywood Sign
EAST CHEVY CHASE DRIVE
Paperback Brewing
GOLDEN STATE FREEWAY
SAN FERNANDO ROAD
Forest Lawn Memorial Park
Griffith Observatory
Hail Mary
ATWATER VILLAGE
LOS FELIZ BOULEVARD
LOS FELIZ
UCB Theatre
Zebulon
Skylight Books
HOLLYWOOD FREEWAY
Harvard and Stone
Tabula Rasa Bar
HOLLYWOOD BLVD
Permanent Records
Rockaway Records
Hollyhock House
Vista Theatre
Tiki-Ti
GOLDEN STATE FREEWAY
EAST HOLLYWOOD
Akbar
El Cid
GLENDALE FREEWAY
The Virgil
Intelligentsia
SANTA MONICA BOULEVARD
SILVER LAKE
Cinespia at the Hollywood Forever Cemetery
The Ruby Fruit
L.A. City College Swap Meet
Melody
SUNSET BOULEVARD
Elysian Park
MELROSE AVENUE
Pop Up Home
SOUTH NORMANDIE AVE
HOLLYWOOD FREEWAY
BEVERLY BOULEVARD
VERMONT AVENUE
SUNSET BOULEVARD
Dodger Stadium
ECHO PARK
WEST 3RD STREET
WILSHIRE CENTER
ALVARADO STREET
HARBOR FREEWAY
WESTLAKE
WILSHIRE BOULEVARD
The Prince
KOREATOWN
DOWNTOWN

EAT

DRINK

SHOP

ARTS & CULTURE

NIGHTLIFE

OUTDOORS

HOLLYWOOD HILLS
0 kilometers 1
0 miles 1
MULHOLLAND DRIVE
HOLLYWOOD FREEWAY
Mulholland Drive
Runyon Canyon
HOLLYWOOD HILLS WEST
LAUREL CANYON BOULEVARD
The Ford
Hollywood Bowl
Runyon Canyon Park
Wattles Garden Park
TROUSDALE ESTATES
The Magic Castle
HOLLYWOO
Black Rabbit Ro
Hollywood Walk of Fame
HOLLYWOOD BOULEVARD
Egyptian Theatre
Laugh Factory
WEST SUNSET BOULEVARD
Saddle Ranch Chop House
The Comedy Store
Skybar
FOUNTAIN AVENUE
NORTH HIGHLAND AVE
Fan Girl Cafe
SANTA MONICA BOULEVARD
The Roxy
WEST SUNSET BOULEVARD
Book Soup
WEST HOLLYWOOD
Schindler House
Hi Tops
The Abbey
E.P. and L.P.
Wild Style LA
Blu Jam Cafe
The Groundlings Theatre
Providen
Troubadour
Decades
Reformation
Milk Bar
Shulamit Nazarian
ONE Gallery
The Hundreds
FAIRFAX
RipNDip
SANTA MONICA BOULEVARD
BEVERLY BOULEVARD
The Roger Room
BEVERLY BOULEVARD
New Beverly Cinema
BEVERLY HILLS
BURTON WAY
A.O.C.
BEVERLY GROVE
The Original Farmers' Market
HANCOCK PARK
FAIRFAX AVENUE
SOUTH LA BREA AVENUE
ROBERTSON BOULEVARD
LA BREA
WILSHIRE BLVD
LA CIENEGA BOULEVARD
Academy Museum
Urban Light
République
Craft Contemporary
WEST OLYMPIC BOULEVARD
WEST OLYMPIC BOULEVARD
WEST PICO BOULEVARD
SAN VICENTE BOULEVARD
MID-WILSHIRE

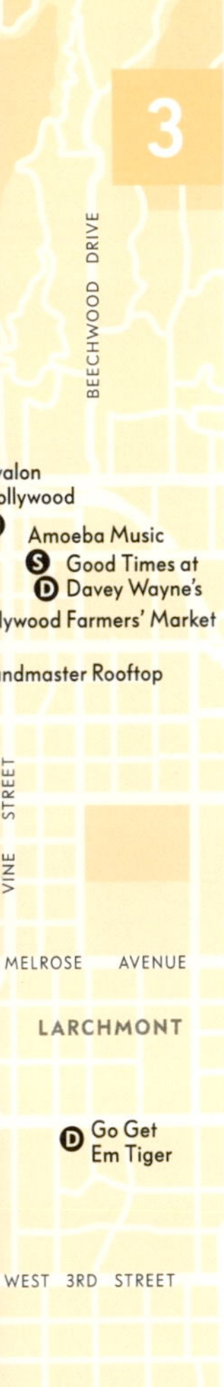

E EAT

Blu Jam Cafe *(p32)*

Milk Bar *(p49)*

Providence *(p44)*

République *(p34)*

D DRINK

A.O.C. *(p75)*

E.P. and L.P. *(p68)*

Fan Girl Cafe *(p61)*

Go Get Em Tiger *(p60)*

Good Times at Davey Wayne's *(p65)*

Grandmaster Rooftop *(p68)*

The Roger Room *(p64)*

S SHOP

Amoeba Music *(p93)*

Book Soup *(p98)*

Decades *(p81)*

Hollywood Farmers' Market *(p102)*

The Hundreds *(p82)*

The Original Farmers' Market *(p102)*

The Record Parlour *(p92)*

Reformation *(p82)*

RipNDip *(p83)*

Wild Style LA *(p81)*

A ARTS & CULTURE

Academy Museum *(p115)*

Craft Contemporary *(p113)*

Egyptian Theatre *(p124)*

The Ford *(p130)*

New Beverly Cinema *(p125)*

ONE Gallery *(p108)*

Schindler House *(p122)*

Shulamit Nazarian *(p130)*

Urban Light *(p116)*

N NIGHTLIFE

The Abbey *(p148)*

Avalon Hollywood *(p155)*

Black Rabbit Rose *(p139)*

The Comedy Store *(p141)*

The Groundlings Theatre *(p142)*

Hi Tops *(p149)*

Hollywood Bowl *(p146)*

Laugh Factory *(p142)*

The Magic Castle *(p137)*

The Roxy *(p147)*

Saddle Ranch Chop House *(p139)*

Skybar *(p154)*

Troubadour *(p146)*

O OUTDOORS

Hollywood Walk of Fame *(p178)*

Mulholland Drive *(p180)*

Runyon Canyon *(p168)*

BEVERLY HILLS
WESTWOOD
Crustacean
MID-WILSHIRE
WILSHIRE BOULEVARD
SUNSET BOULEVARD
SANTA MONICA BLVD
SAN VICENTE BOULEVARD
BRENTWOOD
Saffron & Rose
Attari
WEST SAN VICENTE BLVD
WEST PICO BOULEVARD
Catch One
Mateo's
BEVERLYWOOD
B Sweet Dessert Bar
Coffee Tomo
VENICE BLVD
MID CITY
Record Surplus
SAWTELLE
Museum of Jurassic Technology
HD Buttercup
Compartés
SANTA MONICA FREEWAY
Bru's Wiffle
Band of Vices
SANTA MONICA
SANTA MONICA FREEWAY
SAN DIEGO FREEWAY
Hi-Lo
N/naka
Reparation Club
Mélisse
Margot
The Ripped Bodice
Esters Wine Shop & Bar
Culver City Stairs
Harvelle's
Santa Monica Farmers' Market
BUNDY DRIVE
CULVER CITY
Rolling Greens
LA CIENEGA BOULEVARD
LA BREA AVENUE
Post & Beam
LINCOLN BOULEVARD
MAR VISTA
Mar Vista Farmers' Market
Art + Practic
South Beach Santa Monica
Sunny Blue
Destination Crenshaw
VENICE
VENICE BOULEVARD
Bombay Frankie Company
HYDE PARK
High Rooftop
MARINA FREEWAY
CRENSHAW BOULEVARD
Venice Beach
MARINA DEL REY
PLAYA VISTA
Foodminati's The Court Cafe
Hilltop Coffee + Kitchen
Residency Art Gallery
WEST MANCHESTER AVENUE
Berbere Imports
INGLEWOOD
Football at SoFi Stadiur
VISTA DEL MAR
WESTCHESTER
Los Angeles International Airport
LENNOX
Dockweiler State Beach
CENTURY FREEWAY
EL SEGUNDO
HAWTHORNE
El Segundo Beach
EAST EL SEGUNDO BOULEVARD
PRAIRIE AVENUE
CRENSHAW BOULEVARD
Santa Monica Bay
ROSECRANS AVENUE
Bruce's Beach
LAWNDALE
MANHATTAN BEACH
MANHATTAN BEACH BOULEVARD
REDONDO BEA
0 kilometers 3
0 miles 3
HERMOSA BEACH
ARTESIA BOULEVARD
Hermosa City Beach
LA FRE

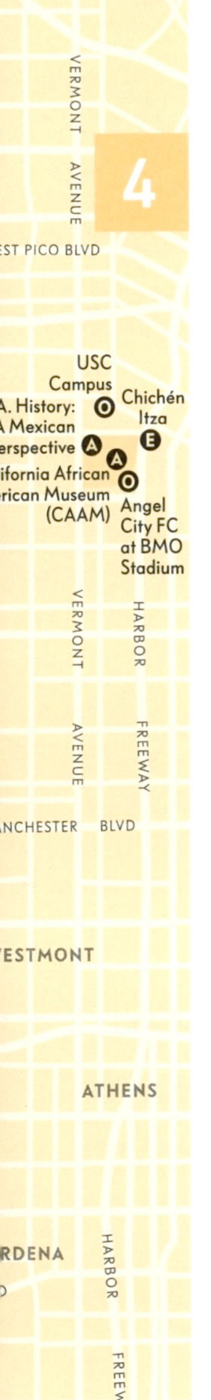

E EAT

Attari *(p43)*

Bombay Frankie Company *(p43)*

Bru's Wiffle *(p35)*

B Sweet Dessert Bar *(p48)*

Chichén Itza *(p43)*

Compartés *(p51)*

Crustacean *(p47)*

Foodminati's The Court Cafe *(p32)*

Mateo's *(p48)*

Mélisse *(p45)*

N/naka *(p44)*

Post & Beam *(p46)*

Saffron & Rose *(p51)*

Sunny Blue *(p40)*

D DRINK

Coffee Tomo *(p60)*

Esters Wine Shop & Bar *(p74)*

High Rooftop *(p69)*

Hilltop Coffee + Kitchen *(p62)*

Hi-Lo *(p73)*

Margot *(p70)*

S SHOP

Berbere Imports *(p91)*

HD Buttercup *(p89)*

Mar Vista Farmers' Market *(p100)*

Record Surplus *(p92)*

Reparations Club *(p98)*

The Ripped Bodice *(p99)*

Rolling Greens *(p88)*

Santa Monica Farmers' Market *(p100)*

A ARTS & CULTURE

Art + Practice *(p129)*

Band of Vices *(p131)*

California African American Museum (CAAM) *(p110)*

Destination Crenshaw *(p117)*

L.A. History: A Mexican Perspective *(p119)*

Museum of Jurassic Technology *(p112)*

Residency Art Gallery *(p130)*

N NIGHTLIFE

Catch One *(p149)*

Harvelle's *(p136)*

O OUTDOORS

Angel City FC at BMO Stadium *(p173)*

Bruce's Beach *(p161)*

Culver City Stairs *(p169)*

Dockweiler State Beach *(p163)*

Football at SoFi Stadium *(p172)*

South Beach Santa Monica *(p162)*

USC Campus *(p178)*

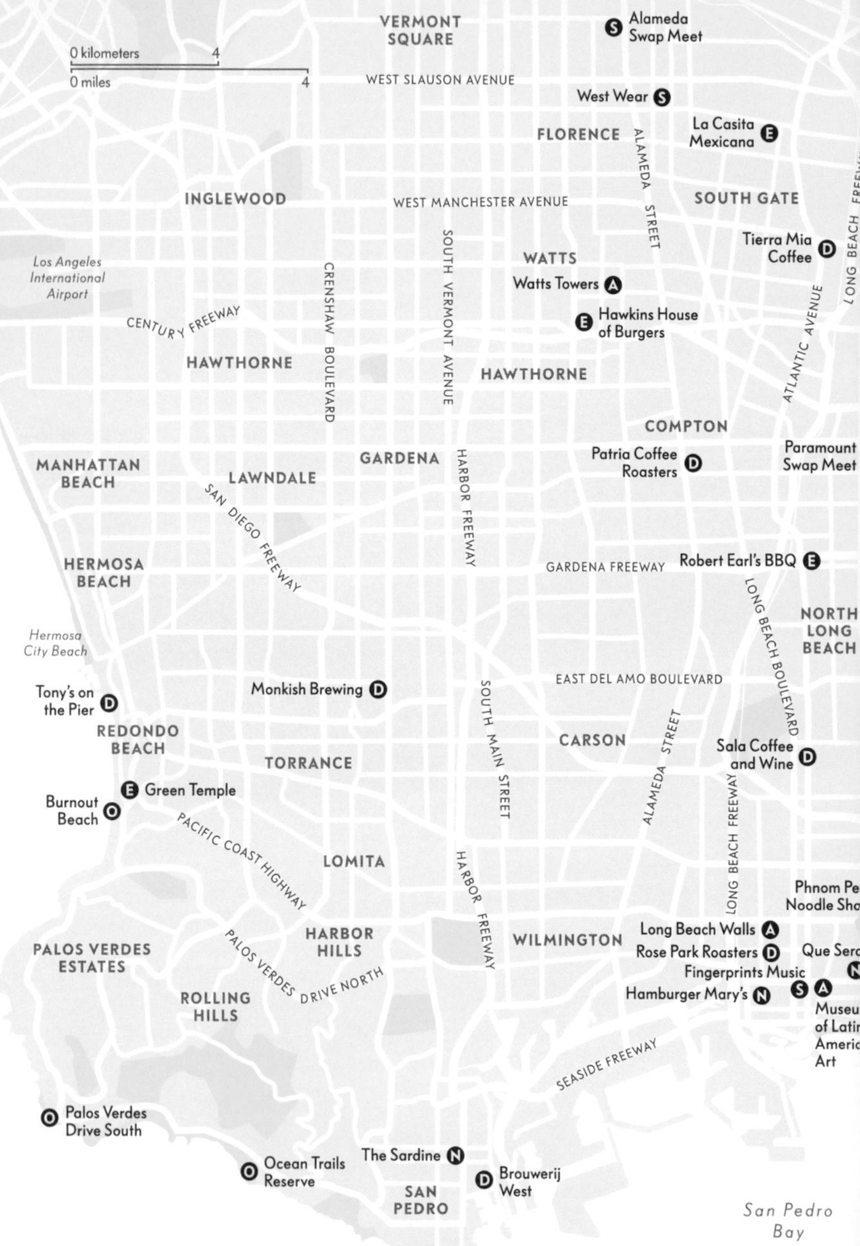

VERMONT SQUARE
Alameda Swap Meet
0 kilometers 4
0 miles 4
WEST SLAUSON AVENUE
West Wear
FLORENCE
La Casita Mexicana
ALAMEDA STREET
INGLEWOOD
WEST MANCHESTER AVENUE
SOUTH GATE
LONG BEACH FREEWAY
Tierra Mia Coffee
SOUTH VERMONT AVENUE
WATTS
Los Angeles International Airport
CRENSHAW BOULEVARD
Watts Towers
Hawkins House of Burgers
CENTURY FREEWAY
ATLANTIC AVENUE
HAWTHORNE
HAWTHORNE
COMPTON
Patria Coffee Roasters
Paramount Swap Meet
MANHATTAN BEACH
GARDENA
HARBOR FREEWAY
LAWNDALE
SAN DIEGO FREEWAY
HERMOSA BEACH
GARDENA FREEWAY
Robert Earl's BBQ
LONG BEACH BOULEVARD
NORTH LONG BEACH
Hermosa City Beach
EAST DEL AMO BOULEVARD
SOUTH MAIN STREET
Tony's on the Pier
Monkish Brewing
REDONDO BEACH
CARSON
ALAMEDA STREET
Sala Coffee and Wine
TORRANCE
LONG BEACH FREEWAY
Green Temple
Burnout Beach
PACIFIC COAST HIGHWAY
LOMITA
HARBOR FREEWAY
Long Beach Walls
HARBOR HILLS
WILMINGTON
Rose Park Roasters
PALOS VERDES ESTATES
PALOS VERDES DRIVE NORTH
Fingerprints Music
Hamburger Mary's
ROLLING HILLS
SEASIDE FREEWAY
Palos Verdes Drive South
Ocean Trails Reserve
The Sardine
Brouwerij West
SAN PEDRO
San Pedro Bay

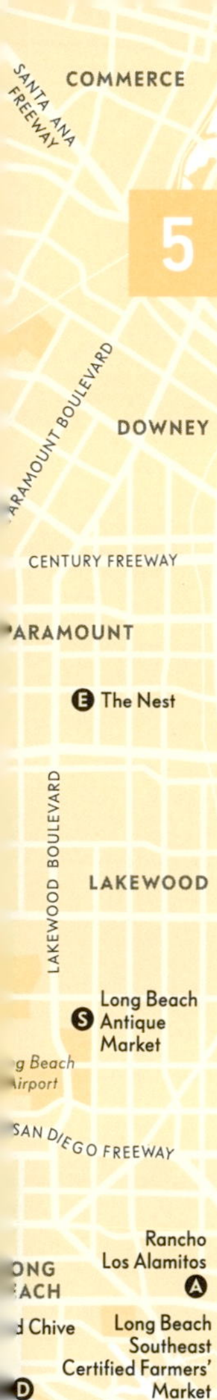

EAT

Green Temple *(p33)*

Hawkins House of Burgers *(p36)*

La Casita Mexicana *(p38)*

The Nest *(p35)*

Phnom Penh Noodle Shack *(p35)*

Robert Earl's BBQ *(p37)*

Wild Chive *(p34)*

DRINK

Belmont Brewing Company *(p70)*

Brouwerij West *(p58)*

Monkish Brewing *(p57)*

Patria Coffee Roasters *(p61)*

Rose Park Roasters *(p63)*

Sala Coffee and Wine *(p73)*

Tierra Mia Coffee *(p62)*

Tony's on the Pier *(p69)*

SHOP

Alameda Swap Meet *(p84)*

Fingerprints Music *(p94)*

Long Beach Antique Market *(p85)*

Long Beach Southeast Certified Farmers' Market *(p101)*

Paramount Swap Meet *(p86)*

West Wear *(p80)*

ARTS & CULTURE

Long Beach Walls *(p119)*

Museum of Latin American Art *(p113)*

Rancho Los Alamitos *(p108)*

Watts Towers *(p116)*

NIGHTLIFE

Hamburger Mary's *(p148)*

Que Sera *(p150)*

The Sardine *(p144)*

OUTDOORS

Burnout Beach *(p161)*

Ocean Boulevard *(p180)*

Ocean Trails Reserve *(p163)*

Palos Verdes Drive South *(p181)*

Peninsula Bayside Beach *(p160*

PALMDALE
CA-14
SANTA CLARITA
I-5
Tía Chucha's Centro Cultural & Bookstore S
SAN FERNANDO
SIMI VALLEY
CA-118
Mural Mile A
Angeles Crest Highway O
NORTHRIDGE
SUN VALLEY
Descanso Gardens O
I-210
The Great Wall of Los Angeles A
Stough Canyon O
Highway 101
30 miles (50 km)
MacLeod Ale Brewing Company D
Flappers N
Rose Bowl Game O
Rose Bowl Flea Market S
Tavern Tomoko & Ladyface Brewery D
Cici's Cafe E
VAN NUYS
Circus Liquor O
Porto's Bakery E
The Gamble Hou
US-101
Wisdom Tree Hike O
Warner Bros Studio Tour O
Gold Bug S
Vroman's S
Freakbeat Records S
Studio City Farmers' Market S
Smoke House E
Hunting Library O
Leaf and Spine S
Big Budd Press S
Blind Barber D
Nucleus A
Santa Monica Mountains
TOPANGA
Ernest E. Debs Park O
Heritage Square Museum A
Leo Carrillo State Park
7 miles (11 km)
Los Liones O
I-405
Bánh Mì My-T
DOWNTOWN
MALIBU
Solstice Canyon O
Pacific Coast Highway O
SANTA MONICA
I-10
Vincent Price Art Museum A
CULVER CITY
Turnbull Canyon
Zuma Beach O
Point Dume O
VENICE
See maps 1–5
for Central Los Angeles
I-5
SOUTHGATE
DOWNEY
INGLEWOOD
WATTS
I-105
Santa Monica Bay
HAWTHORNE
Santa Fe Springs Swap Meet
COMPTON
REDONDO BEACH
I-405
TORRANCE
CARSON
SIGNAL HILL
LONG BEACH
PALOS VERDES
NAPLES
SAN PEDRO
Beachwoo BBQ & Brewin
San Pedro Bay
0 kilometers 10
0 miles 10

6

Chantry Flat
Joshua Tree National Park
125 miles (200 km)
I-210
Chatterbox Comedy
EL MONTE
COVINA
I-10
The Donut Hole
CA-60
Palms to Pines Scenic Byway
95 miles (155 km)
LA HABRA
FULLERTON
CA-91
I-5
ANAHEIM
The Frida Cinema
CA-22
SANTA ANA
I-405
Huntington Beach
COSTA MESA

EAT

DRINK

SHOP

ARTS & CULTURE

NIGHTLIFE

OUTDOORS

EAT

Slurp Cambodian soup for breakfast, snack on Mexican tacos for lunch, and savor Korean BBQ for dinner – L.A. offers endless culinary delights, bursting with global flavors.

Brunch Spots

In Los Angeles, brunch is celebrated like a religion, with top destinations filling up faster than a Sunday service. It's a ritual faithfully observed by all – obligatory glass of mimosa firmly in hand.

BLU JAM CAFE

Map 3; 7371 Melrose Avenue, West Hollywood; ///steps.packet.final; www.blujamcafe.com

For a classic L.A. brunch experience, look no further than Blu Jam. Here, hearty portions of organic Benedicts, overstuffed omelets, and Mexican staples like chilaquiles are served alongside a carefully curated selection of coffees. There are now seven locations around the city (always packed with a crowd), but the Melrose Avenue original is still our favorite for a weekend group hang.

FOODMINATI'S THE COURT CAFE

Map 4; 5496 W. Centinela Avenue, Westchester; ///mice.complains.rally; (310) 431-4969

What more fitting headquarters for a (not-so-) secret food society than a low-key café in a nondescript strip mall? Founded by a pair of chefs with cult followings on social media, it's a chamber of culinary

Check out The Court Cafe's Instagram feed to discover why the chefs have a devoted social media following.

wonders – think lobster and waffles, taco omelets, and decadent French toast sandwiches. What better way to start a lazy Sunday?

GREEN TEMPLE

Map 5; 1700 S. Catalina Avenue, Redondo Beach; ///tins.rope.cage; www.greentemple.net

Any thoughts of traffic-filled freeways are soon banished at this beachside vegetarian haven. Its leafy patio is the hideaway of health-conscious South Bay locals, who catch up over the soothing soundtrack of a burbling koi-filled fountain. Dishes on the eclectic menu range from walnut loaf to Asian-influenced veggie bowls, all washed down with a mandatory glass of frothy green juice. It's enough to get anyone a bit closer to finding inner peace.

CICI'S CAFE

Map 6; 18912 Ventura Boulevard, Tarzana; ///books.drips.claps; www.ciciscafe.com

Drawing hordes of hungry patrons from across the San Fernando Valley, the menu at Cici's will satisfy even the most demanding sweet tooth. There are 80 (yes, 80) different pancake varieties, nearly all of which come topped with whipped cream. For first-timers, the green tea tiramisu or chocolate velvet options are safe and scrumptious bets.

» **Don't leave without** trying the pillowy soufflé pancakes. Trust us, they're a decadent treat to die for.

WILD CHIVE

Map 5; 2650 E. Broadway, Long Beach; ///riches.dazzling.same; www.thewildchive.com

After years of serving her mouthwatering vegan brunches through pop-ups, chef Soozee Nguyen finally landed her own brick-and-mortar establishment. Great news for Long Beach regulars (and visitors), who can now wolf down her meat-free Monte Cristos, mushroom burgers, and breakfast banh mi whenever they want.

RÉPUBLIQUE

Map 3; 624 S. La Brea Avenue, Hancock Park; ///bats.freed.froth; www.republiquela.com

Husband-and-wife chef team Walter and Margarita Manzke run a veritable food empire, including buzzy Filipino counter Sari Sari Store and upscale Parisian bistro La Bicyclette. But République is where it all started. While the dinner menu here gets the most hype, weekend brunch is where it really shines brightest: Walter's French-influenced dishes match perfectly with Margarita's fresh breads and pastries.

Try it!
PICNIC BRUNCH

The Saturday farmers' market in downtown Santa Monica offers an incredible selection of flaky organic pastries. Grab a mix of sweet and savory treats and wander down to the beach for a picnic brunch.

BRU'S WIFFLE

Map 4; 2408 Wilshire Boulevard, Santa Monica; ///puzzle.spite.occurs; (310) 453-2787

Everyone from movie execs to college students battles for tables at this Westside chicken-and-waffle joint. Of course, the go-to is anything involving fried chicken and a waffle, but the loaded avocado toast and truffle oil eggs are equally tempting.

THE NEST

Map 5; 16916 Bellflower Blvd, Bellflower; ///spoon.briefing.glee; www.eatnest.com

It's fair to say the remote suburb of Bellflower is not one of L.A.'s top foodie hot spots. Thanks to this friendly Latinx breakfast joint, however, that's set to change. Making its name are standout dishes like the churro waffle and the breakfast poutine – oh, and the iced coffees are a caffeine addict's dream.

PHNOM PENH NOODLE SHACK

Map 5; 1644 Cherry Avenue, Long Beach; ///menu.fight.included; www.thenoodleshack.com

Fun fact: Long Beach is reportedly home to the largest population of Cambodians outside Southeast Asia. And where better to start exploring the community's heritage than this quick-fire Cambodian soup joint. Noodles for breakfast? Yes, please.

» **Don't leave without** ordering *kuyteav*, a traditional Cambodian breakfast soup served with a pork bone broth.

Comfort Food

Like much else in L.A.'s culture, what qualifies as comfort food breaks all the rules. Instead of hearty soups and stews, Angelenos find cheer in a mix of nostalgic standbys that soothe the soul.

HOWLIN' RAY'S

Map 1; 727 N. Broadway #128, Chinatown; ///punt.glee.smashes; www.howlinrays.com

Inspired by the punchy heat of Nashville's famous hot chicken, this cramped counter in Chinatown's foodie Far East Plaza was the pioneer behind L.A.'s Southern sandwich craze. The lines are forever long (no less than an hour, be prepared for up to five) and the fried chicken almost sparkles with fiery red spice, but you'll undoubtedly find yourself desperate for more.

HAWKINS HOUSE OF BURGERS

Map 5; 11603 Slater Street, Watts; ///dream.palm.wants; www.hawkinsburgers.com

You'd think the monstrous burgers at Hawkins were invented to be Instagrammed, but it was back in 1939 that James Henry Hawkins started slinging his signature patties. Each burger is built on a foundation of craggy, half-pound Angus, pristinely charred at the edges and densely wrapped in toppings as tame as tomato and lettuce and as intense as hot links, pastrami, and eggs. Served from a building smooshed against the 105 Freeway, they're a favorite with neighbors from the public housing projects across the street.

ROBERT EARL'S BBQ

Map 5; 703 Artesia Boulevard, Long Beach; ///form.serve.snipe; www.robertearlsbbq.com

For most of his adult life, Robert Earl was a backyard pit master, serving slow-smoked Texas-style dishes at family gatherings and catering gigs alongside the day job. In 2012, he started rolling his smoker over to his hometown farmers' market and – one award-winning brick-and-mortar roadhouse later – the rest is L.A. BBQ history.

PHILIPPE THE ORIGINAL

Map 1; 1001 N. Alameda Street, Downtown; ///voters.pinks.souk; www.philippes.com

The fight over who invented the French dip is as old and heated as L.A. itself. Look, every version of this jus-dipped roast beef sandwich is delicious, but when it comes to an experience that's as comforting as the food, Philippe's is the clear winner. Since 1908, lunch here has been an L.A. rite of passage for everyone, from downtown construction workers to fresh-faced arrivals from nearby Union Station.

» **Don't leave without** ordering a second sandwich. The roast beef is legendary, but there's also lamb, turkey, pastrami, pork, and ham.

LA CASITA MEXICANA

Map 5; 4030 E. Gage Avenue, Bell; ///oddly.crowned.mixed; www.casitamex.com

It's hard to imagine a Mexican food scene in L.A. without Jaime Martin del Campo and Ramiro Arvizu, the celebrity chef duo who opened La Casita Mexicana in 1999. This place is truly iconic, serving regional specialties with immense love and pride.

» **Don't leave without** ordering the *chile en nogada* (chilies in walnut sauce), a classic dish that incorporates the colors of the Mexican flag.

HAIL MARY

Map 2; 3219 Glendale Boulevard, Atwater; ///saying.turns.silent; www.hailmarypizzala.com

Forget the pies of New York and Chicago. L.A.'s pizza scene has grown out of the city's artisanal bakeries, and you can taste the difference in the dough. Hail Mary is a great place to try this new crust culture, with its signature sourdough base and seasonal toppings.

POLKA POLISH CUISINE

Map 2; 4112 Verdugo Road, Glassel Park; ///stands.purely.cafe; www.polkarestaurant.com

Don't have a Polish grandmother to make you piping hot pierogi? Homey Polka has you covered. Founded by two Polish expats with a heart for their homeland's cuisine, this modest strip mall joint is a mainstay for nostalgic Eastern Europeans and young Eastsiders looking for a hug on a plate.

Liked by the locals

"I wanted to make a crust and pizza that I wanted to eat. Naturally leavened sourdough, whole grains, and organic and locally grown ingredients. Nothing fussy, just a commitment to quality."

DAVID WILCOX,
HAIL MARY OWNER

Quick Bites

As laid-back as L.A. is, spending your life stuck in traffic can leave little time for sustenance. Luckily, there are lots of places with rapid-fire service that can whip up a great meal in minutes.

SUNNY BLUE

Map 4; 12608 W. Washington Boulevard, Culver City; ///spice.fend.grass; www.sunnyblueinc.com

If you want quick but also delish, you can't beat the highly snackable *omusubi* (Japanese rice balls) at this small Culver City counter. On any weekday afternoon you'll find studio workers stocking up on the handcrafted morsels, stuffed with crowd-pleasing fillings like kara tuna, miso beef, and sautéed eggplant with chili miso. Can't decide? Nothing on the menu is more than $5, so just get one of everything.

BÁNH MÌ MY-THO

Map 6; 304 W. Valley Boulevard, Rosemead; ///rounds.punk.sulk; www.banhmimytho.com

Admittedly, this San Gabriel gem isn't the top choice if you're in a genuine hurry – it's a bit of a drive and you'll likely have to wait in the inevitable line – but its Vietnamese banh mi are so good you'll

Remember to hit up the ATM on your way to Bánh Mì My-Tho; the small shop is cash only.

wolf them down in seconds. Think generously sized portions of flavorful meat or tofu, drizzled with spicy aioli and tightly wrapped inside a cloud-soft bun.

EL PARIAN

Map 1; 1528 W. Pico Boulevard, Downtown; ///gender.causes.shell; (213) 386-7361

Birria (stewed goat) tacos are having an indisputable moment in the L.A. food scene, with more and more trucks serving up the fat-dipped Jaliscan specialty. But this family-owned institution is no trend hopper. They're veterans in the game, preparing birria for loyal regulars and in-the-know enthusiasts for nearly 50 years. It's the real deal, right down to the ranchera music trickling out of the jukebox.

SONORATOWN

Map 1; 208 E. 8th Street, Downtown; ///lend.thinks.dairy; www.sonoratown.com

When restaurateurs Teodoro Diaz-Rodriguez Jr. and Jennifer Feltham opened this joint, the pair had one mission: to serve traditional north Mexican tacos, stuffed with perfectly prepared carne asada. It's safe to say they nailed it – this restaurant is regularly packed with downtown office dwellers and Latinx neighbors enjoying fat burritos and tangy salsa roja.

» **Don't leave without** buying a bag of homemade flour tortillas – they're some of the best in the city and sold to-go if you ask.

Solo, Pair, Crowd

There's a taco truck for every occasion in L.A., whether you're fueling up solo or feasting with friends.

FLYING SOLO

Eat on the fly

Ricky's Fish Tacos, with its mean crispy fish with smoky, spicy red salsa, makes a great grab-and-go lunch for one. Check Twitter to find out where the truck will be each day.

IN A PAIR

Lunchtime date

Mariscos Jalisco is very no frills and that's the way we like it, thank you very much. This lunch truck (there are five around the city) is great for a budget-friendly day date. Order a selection of ceviche tostadas to share.

FOR A CROWD

Feast with friends

If you like dipping delicious things into other delicious things, then Teddy's Red Tacos is for you. Bring some friends and feast on birria consomé tacos at one of the city's 10 Teddy's trucks.

ATTARI

Map 4; 1388 Westwood Boulevard, Little Tehran; ///learns.analogy.crowd; www.attarisandwiches.com

Tucked away off the trafficky Westwood Boulevard, this sandwich shop is one of Little Tehran's best-kept secrets. You won't find classic cold cuts here – instead, the Persian expats and occasional UCLA students lunching in its tree-lined courtyard come for the tongue and brain sandwich (trust us), finished off with a bite of baklava.

CHICHÉN ITZA

Map 4; 3655 S. Grand Avenue c6, Downtown; ///album.robots.king; www.chichenitzarestaurant.com

Chef Gilberto Cetina opened this joint in 2001, and since then has enjoyed nonstop acclaim for his Yucatán-inspired fare. The humble counter serves up amazing *cochinita pibil* (slow-roasted pork tacos) that will linger in your mind long after your lunch is over.

BOMBAY FRANKIE COMPANY

Map 4; 6000 Sepulveda Boulevard Suite 1601, Culver City; ///indeed.flood.liked; www.thebombayfrankiecompany.com

The brainchild of an Indian American brother-sister duo raised in L.A., this Indian burrito spot started life as a side offering at a gas station. Now in a stand-alone space in the Westfield Mall, it's still attracting a devoted following with its tasty modern street food.

» **Don't leave without** trying the crowd-pleasing chicken tikka masala Frankie (Indian burrito), wrapped in tandoor-baked garlic naan.

Special Occasion

L.A. may not be inundated with Michelin stars, but that doesn't mean the city lacks in fine dining. These celebration-worthy spots focus on chef-driven food, elevating the eating experience beyond the everyday.

PROVIDENCE

Map 3; 5955 Melrose Avenue, Hollywood; ///spices.hobby.skill; www.providencela.com

Just because you have a Michelin star or two, doesn't mean you have to be showy. For almost 20 years, this Hollywood hideaway has been quietly luring well-heeled regulars with the simple promise of the city's finest sustainable seafood. Yes, you might have to forgo this month's rent money to eat here, but the epic eight-course tasting menu is totally worth it.

N/NAKA

Map 4; 3455 Overland Avenue, Palms; ///slime.margin.fall; www.n-naka.com

Okay, you'll need perseverance and/or luck to get a table here (there are only 26 seats and reservations disappear in seconds), but hang on in there until you do. Chef Nikki Naka's California take on Japanese *kaiseki* – a traditional dinner of small plates, featuring locally grown, seasonal ingredients – is an utterly exquisite experience. If you're tempted to rejoin the reservation queue, do – she famously never serves guests the same dish twice.

MÉLISSE

Map 4; 1104 Wilshire Boulevard, Santa Monica; ///trial.anyway.pools; www.citrinandmelisse.com

Snobby scenesters might see this restaurant's white tablecloths and formal decor as stuffy, but Mélisse clearly isn't concerned about keeping up with design trends. And why would it, when dishes like clam chowder custard and coffee-crusted lamb have won it two Michelin stars? The intimate setting makes this a great place to celebrate an anniversary (just book in advance).

BESTIA

Map 1; 2121 E. 7th Place, Arts District; ///exact.sticks.format; www.bestiala.com

The 2012 launch of this too-cool Italian restaurant single-handedly revived the Arts District food scene – and it's been a battle to snag a table here ever since. Thankfully, despite its reputation, the swanky joint still manages to feel approachable and inviting, its industrial-chic dining room humming with the chatter of lucky local creatives as they catch up over plates of the city's best pasta.

» **Don't leave without** trying something from the impressive wine list – all bottles are biodynamic.

POST & BEAM

Map 4; 3767 Santa Rosalia Drive, Leimert Park; ///food.equal.full; www.postandbeamla.com

As you step onto the verdant patio of Post & Beam, the twinkly porch lights, fragrant herb garden, and live R&B music immediately make you forget you're in a city. And the homey atmosphere only gets cozier as you tuck into the elevated Southern cooking. Traditional soul food like shrimp and grits or honey cornbread is front and center here, as part of a menu celebrating Black heritage.

SMOKE HOUSE

Map 6; 4420 Lakeside Drive, Burbank; ///pouch.listed.email; www.smokehouse1946.com

Since opening its doors down the street from the Warner Bros. studio in 1946, this hangout has remained an industry favorite. The dark, cozy atmosphere has ensnared legions of famous fans, from

Run by the owners of Post & Beam, Black Pot Supper Club *(www.postandbeamla.com/hemings-hercules)* is South L.A.'s only outdoor dinner series celebrating historic African American cuisine. Snag a reservation at one of these intimate events to experience chef Martin Draluck's spectacular eight course dinner, accompanied by a short speech about the food's historical importance.

Judy Garland and James Dean to George Clooney (who named his production company after it). Settle into the classic red leather booths and savor solid steakhouse staples like prime rib and lobster tail.

» **Don't leave without** ordering the famous garlic cheese bread. As all regulars know, it's not a visit to the Smoke House without it.

ORSA & WINSTON

Map 1; 122 W. 4th Street, Downtown; ///modern.grows.desk; www.orsaandwinston.com

Although Orsa & Winston is on the splurge-y end of chef Josef Centeno's downtown foodie empire (he's up to four restaurants so far), you can still treat yourself without breaking the bank. For $125, you'll receive a five-course tasting menu inspired by Italian and Japanese flavors – though it's usually closer to 10, with all the in-between amuse-bouches that float out from the kitchen.

CRUSTACEAN

Map 4; 468 N. Bedford Drive, Beverly Hills; ///salsa.crash.fleet; www.crustaceanbh.com

After fleeing Saigon in 1971, the An family went on to pioneer the modern Vietnamese food movement in San Francisco, before bringing their talents to Beverly Hills. Their much-loved L.A. institution has long sat at the top of the seafood scene, with the roasted king crab and garlic noodles becoming legends in their own right. It's a fave with Hollywood A-listers and the Beverly Hills elite, as proven by the not-so-subtle paparazzi milling about outside.

Sweet Treats

Pastry chefs and ice-cream shops and sugary drinks, oh my! L.A. is a hotbed of sweets and desserts, thanks to a creative fusion of immigrant traditions and dishes designed for drool-worthy social media posts.

MATEO'S

Map 4; 4234 Pico Boulevard, Mid City; ///sticks.finest.thus; www.mateosicecreamla.com

Usually, the best Mexican ice-cream stores in L.A. have "Michoacana" in the name, a nod to the Mexican state famed for its traditional creamy desserts. But this mini chain of strip mall shops is the exception that proves the rule. Our favorite location is the first-ever store in Mid City, where local families are lured by dozens of tempting flavors, piles of fresh fruits, and a rainbow of *paletas* (Mexican popsicles).

B SWEET DESSERT BAR

Map 4; 2005 Sawtelle Boulevard, Sawtelle; ///liked.analogy.hotels; www.mybsweet.com

Ever since her humble food truck beginnings, self-taught chef Barb Batiste has been at the forefront of L.A.'s Filipino food movement. Inspired by her mother's home cooking (from the heart, no

Cans of B Sweet's signature cold brew coffee and sugar-free teas are sold in many health food stores.

measurements, lots of purple yam), she doles out her famous bread puddings, seasonal cheesecakes, and still-moist cookies in portions built to share.

FUGETSU-DO CONFECTIONERY

Map 1; 315 E. 1st Street, Little Tokyo; ///also.shell.gains; www.fugetsu-do.com

Specializing in the taffy-like mochi, this Japanese confectionery has been a mainstay of Little Tokyo for more than a hundred years. Its third-generation owner, Brian Kito, is a master mochi craftsman who uses a mix of rice, gelatin, and flour to execute impossible feats of color, texture, and flavor. Each piece is a delicate masterpiece that's almost too good-looking to eat (but no, really, you should eat it).

» Don't leave without trying both classic mochi, filled with bean paste, and *ogura*, which flips the mochi inside out with a bean paste exterior.

MILK BAR

Map 3; 7150 Melrose Avenue, Fairfax; ///flames.envy.intro; www.milkbarstore.com

Don't be put off by the perpetual line: the goodies inside Milk Bar's West Coast flagship are as sweet as its pink decor. And the line is all part of the fun, anyway. Not only do you get to peek inside the bakery's combination classroom, commissary, and R&D lab, but you get plenty of time to ogle the small but formidable menu of addictive shakes, cakes, and truffles. The hardest part of the whole experience is narrowing down what to order.

Solo, Pair, Crowd

I scream, you scream, we all scream for somewhere to eat ice cream – thankfully, L.A. has plenty of options.

FLYING SOLO

Filipino quick fix

Satisfy that sweet tooth at one of L.A.'s few Jollibees (a Filipino fast-food chain). The halo-halo, a decadent dessert layered with beans, ice, and condensed milk, is a go-to.

IN A PAIR

A taste of Italy

Impress your date by transporting them to a classic Italian gelateria – without ever leaving the Valley. It's here that the famous Italian chain Fatamorgana Gelato opened its first location outside of Rome, serving nearly 70 flavors daily.

FOR A CROWD

Korean classic

Korean shaved ice, aka *bingsoo*, is not designed to be eaten alone. Gather the crew and head to Sul & Beans, where even a small size of this loaded-up dessert will feed a whole party.

PORTO'S BAKERY

Map 1; 3614 W. Magnolia Boulevard, Burbank; ///resort.study.grapes; www.portosbakery.com

A trip to this family-run Cuban bakery (or one of its four sister branches) is like participating in a carefully choreographed ballet. Unending lines of families wait their turn to pick from the glossy cakes and tropical tarts, while dozens of workers dance behind a gleaming counter in an organized chaos that must be seen to be believed.

SAFFRON & ROSE

Map 4; 1387 Westwood Boulevard, Little Tehran; ///broker.spike.blend; www.saffronrosepersianicecream.com

A meeting place for Persian expats, UCLA students, and young Westside families, this ice-cream parlor is the unofficial city hall of Little Tehran. Scoops come in Middle Eastern flavors like pistachio, orange blossom, and, of course, the store's namesake saffron and rose.

» Don't leave without trying a scoop of *faloodeh*, a rosewater-flavored sorbet marbled with rice noodles.

COMPARTÉS

Map 4; 5735 West Adams Blvd, West Adams; ///lied.robot.young; www.compartes.com

Always dreamed of visiting Willy Wonka's chocolate factory? Here's the next best thing. Compartés' gourmet chocolate bars – flecked with everything from sea salt to potato chips – have been luring customers with childlike delight since as far back as the 1950s.

TAKE A TOUR

A foodie afternoon in Koreatown

The 1960s saw record numbers of Koreans move to the West Coast. One such person was Hi Duk Lee, a businessman with a vision. The grocery store owner set out to remedy L.A.'s lack of businesses serving immigrants like him, by buying a block of streets to house Korean-owned stores and restaurants. Today, this patch remains a hub for the community, as well as a hot spot for Korean fare. Spend some hours eating your way around this mini city, which locals say rivals the streets of Seoul.

1. Surawon Tofu House
2833 W. Olympic Boulevard; (213) 383-7317
///yoga.sadly.fund

2. SomiSomi
621 S. Western Avenue #208-A; www.somisomi.com
///relax.wiping.feared

3. Cafe Mak
612 Shatto Place; (213) 252-9898
///hails.flock.fats

4. Quarters Korean BBQ
3465 W. 6th Street #C-130; www.quarterskbbq.com
///pads.spicy.eggs

Olympic Boulevard and Normandie Avenue
///fried.rips.factories

WEST 3RD

Sate your sweet tooth at SOMISOMI

Indulge in a customized *ah-boong*, a fish-shaped waffle cone stuffed with soft-serve ice cream and your choice of colorful toppings (think rainbow sprinkles and mini macarons).

WEST OLYMPI

WEST PICO

Line up at
QUARTERS KOREAN BBQ

Wait it out for a table at this beloved Korean BBQ restaurant, where guests cook their chosen meats on the tableside grill and gorge on an endless stream of *banchan* (assorted pickled snacks).

Linger at
CAFE MAK

This tea and coffee shop serves cups of caffeine a dozen ways. Our top pick? It's between the plum tea and Korean-style coffee.

Start at
SURAWON TOFU HOUSE

Fuel up for the afternoon ahead by tucking into a gurgling pot of *soondubu jjigae*, a spicy soup made with house-made tofu.

Hi Duk Lee purchased streets around **Olympic Boulevard and Normandie Avenue** *as a starting point for Koreatown.*

DRINK

With its classically Californian good weather, L.A. was made for relaxing outdoors with a drink. Sip wine on a sunny patio, drink beer by the beach, or swig coffee in leafy courtyards.

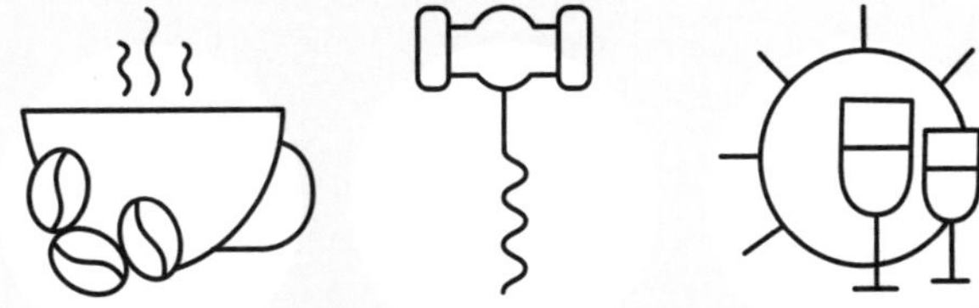

Breweries

For a long time San Diego ruled the SoCal beer scene, but now L.A. is challenging for the crown. With boundary-pushing breweries in every corner of the county, you're never far from a good pint.

HIGHLAND PARK BREWING

Map 1; 1220 N. Spring Street, Chinatown; ///pencil.thanks.verse; hpb.la

It's not only in Hollywood where you'll find a great rags-to-riches story. Highland Park's tale begins in the early days of L.A.'s beer scene, when a humble homebrewer set up shop in the tiny back rooms of a former escort club. With little more than a bathroom drain and space to make only a few kegs at a time, Bob Kunz started creating crisp, sessionable ales and lagers as house brewer for The Hermosillo bar.

Try it!
BREW YOUR OWN

Inspired by L.A.'s homebrewers-turned-pros? You can buy raw materials for making your own beer at the Home Beer Wine Cheesemaking Shop in Woodland Hills *(www.homebeerwinecheese.com)*.

Cut to now, and he's the proud owner of this dedicated downtown tasting room, where the hoppy pilsners and zippy IPAs are the delight of local hipsters.

» Don't leave without trying Hello L.A., Highland Park Brewery's first IPA and a classic balanced-but-bold Los Angeles take on the style.

MONKISH BREWING

Map 5; 20311 S. Western Avenue, Torrance; ///hugs.define.blocks; www.monkishbrewing.com

If you're the kind of person who tracks hype in the craft beer world, Monkish needs no introduction. After launching the brand in 2012 with a focus on Belgian-style beers, brewmaster Henry Nguyen decided to test his talents as a yeast whisperer on an emerging style: the New England IPA. Less like traditional bitter IPAs and closer in flavor to juicy oatmeal pale ales, Monkish's hazy IPAs have become legendary outside L.A. They still have a strong local fan base, mind you, as attested by the beach bums and beer industry workers you'll find in the brewery's taproom.

HOMAGE BREWING

Map 1; 1219 N. Main Street Chinatown; ///noted.field.goods; www.homagebrewing.com

This quirky brewery is a bit of a shapeshifter. One evening you'll walk in to find locals living it up on the dancefloor (a few too many beers deep), another you'll join sports fans watching the game on the screen. You're never quite sure what you're going to get ... but that's half the fun.

ARTS DISTRICT BREWING

Map 1; 828 Traction Avenue, Arts District; ///employ.raced.civic; www.artsdistrictbrewing.com

When Arts District Brewing opened at the end of 2015, L.A. had never seen a tasting room quite like it. Built into a multilevel converted ice house, it features an arcade's worth of Skee-Ball machines and a 100-ft- (30-m-) long central wood bar (with an impressive selection of top-shelf liquor). The beers are as majestic as the cavernous space – hit up your friends and get a crowd together so you can make a proper night of it.

BROUWERIJ WEST

Map 5; 110 E. 22nd Street, Warehouse No. 9, San Pedro; ///genre.unguided.pavers; www.brouwerijwest.com

With its waterfront warehouse setting and annual summer music festival, Brouwerij West positively oozes coastal California cool. And it's not just us who think that – young drinkers flock here from the entire South Bay area, drawn by the funky beers sold in must-collect cans, all designed by local artists.

MACLEOD ALE BREWING COMPANY

Map 6; 14741 Calvert Street, Van Nuys; ///spend.curl.meant; www.macleodale.com

Is that the roil of bagpipes in the distance? Don't worry; you're not imagining things. The owners of MacLeod Ale Brewing Company are members of L.A.'s small but mighty community of Scots and

For a true British pint, order one of the cask ales – they're served in traditional British 20 oz glasses.

started brewing as a way to fund their bagpipe troupe's competitions. Happily for everyone, the beer piped from the kegs is just as melodious as the tunes.

BEACHWOOD BBQ & BREWING

Map 6; 5205 Warner Ave Huntington Beach; ///engine.toenail.nets; www.beachwoodbbq.com

For the majority of its existence, Beachwood BBQ & Brewing's beers have swept every major competition in which they were entered. (Oh, and it was officially named one of the world's best brewpubs at the World Beer Cup in 2016.) But you wouldn't guess it. This low-key spot is reliably laid-back, with a mix of regulars quietly sipping on brash IPAs and savoring artisanal sourdough pizza.

» **Don't leave without** trying the winelike beers from Beachwood Blendery, the Belgian sour ale project around the corner.

PAPERBACK BREWING

Map 2; 422 Magnolia Avenue, Glendale; ///tilt.bumps.legs; paperback.la

Here's the story: two strangers meet over an office email chain and soon realize they have more in common than their jobs in advertising. Two of those things being a love of books and a passion for brewing craft beer. They set up shop in a garage and after years of perfecting their recipes, finally open their own brewery in a World War II airplane hanger. And how about the beer? Packaged in comic book-inspired cans, these tasty brews are worth writing home about.

Coffee Shops

As every Angeleno knows, caffeine is the key to creativity (and, well, happiness in general). From funky college coffee shops to third-wave minimalist joints, here are the best places in the city to find a cup of joe.

COFFEE TOMO

Map 4; 11309 Mississippi Avenue, Sawtelle; ///healthier.bench.lied; (310) 444-9390

Are you at Coffee Tomo for the hand-dripped cup of single-origin joe or the giant artisanal pretzel filled with sweet potatoes and mozzarella? We say come for both. Everything at this gourmet coffee shop is crafted to perfection, from the work-of-art lattes to the calming Japanese design aesthetic.

GO GET EM TIGER

Map3; 230 N. Larchmont Boulevard, Larchmont; ///stove.gear.shovels; www.gget.com

Coffee is more than just a drink in L.A.: it's a way of life. And nowhere is that more true than Go Get Em Tiger (or GGET). Set up by two champion baristas, this rapidly expanding L.A. chain has essentially become its own lifestyle brand. Its hip neighborhood cafés serve carefully curated beans and restaurant-quality food, with a line of branded clothing on the side. Our favorite branch is this one in Larchmont, where the long counter creates a cool, barlike vibe.

» Don't leave without eating something. Each location has its own menu; here, it's all about breakfast goodies like pastries and waffles.

PATRIA COFFEE ROASTERS

Map 5; 108 Alameda Street, Compton; ///courier.manage.audit; www.patriacoffee.com

One of the few independently owned coffee shops amid the sprawling grid of South Los Angeles, Patria is a co-op roastery and retail space that serves its community while supporting it, too. Events like bike rides and film screenings are held here on weekends, but most days you'll find young creatives tapping away on MacBooks, reading the local literary journal (shout out to *Dryland*), and sipping house-roasted beans from across Latin America.

FAN GIRL CAFE

Map 3; 8157 Santa MonicaBoulevard, West Hollywood; ///issues.crush.meals; fangirlcafe.com

They say that a coffee shop can be the heart of a community, and Fan Girl Cafe is living proof. Dedicated to supporting women, non-binary, and LGBTQ+ artists in the music industry, this vibey pink cafe brings the fans together via welcoming open mic nights and album streaming parties. If its buzzy line up of events isn't enough to tempt you, consider the coffee – it's from beloved brand Intelligentsia *(p62)*.

HILLTOP COFFEE + KITCHEN

Map 4; 170 N. La Brea Avenue, Inglewood; ///cabin.speak.froze; www.findyourhilltop.com

South of the 10 Freeway, there aren't a lot of inspiring spaces where people can get creative over a quality brew. That's where Hilltop Coffee + Kitchen comes in. Its first store was such a hit with actress Issa Rae that she partnered with the owners to bring this second location to her hometown of Inglewood. Who knows – as you sip the top-notch coffee, maybe you'll rub shoulders with the creator of the next *Insecure*.

INTELLIGENTSIA

Map 2; 3922 Sunset Boulevard, Silver Lake; ///safely.winter.wrong; www.intelligentsia.com

In 2007, when Intelligentsia opened this Silver Lake flagship, specialty coffee culture was way outside L.A.'s comfort zone. The Chicago-based brand essentially launched the city's third-wave coffee scene, and now it's hard to imagine a time when single-origin hand pours weren't standard. If all the hipsters here are anything to go by, it looks like Intelligentsia's premium craft coffee will be around a while yet.

TIERRA MIA COFFEE

Map 5; 4914 Firestone Boulevard, South Gate; ///jump.decide.alarm; www.tierramiacoffee.com

Who says great coffee has to mean high-concept spaces and prices? Not Tierra Mia. This locally spawned chain is a breath of fresh air, with a proudly Latin vibe that honors the heritage of its beans. Each branch nestles into a historic Latinx neighborhood, repurposing whatever architecture defined the location before (in El Monte, an A-frame Mexican fast-food walk-up; in Long Beach, a former Taco Bell). Shops also have no Wi-Fi, so instead of laptops, you'll find conversations – between *abuelas* and grandkids, and servers and regulars.

» Don't leave without trying Tierra Mia's famous horchata or dulce de leche lattes. They can also be ice blended for a cold buzz.

ROSE PARK ROASTERS

Map 5; 800 Pine Avenue, Long Beach; ///howler.marked.bolts; www.roseparkroasters.com

The philosophy at Rose Park is simple: the best cup of coffee is the one you make at home. The team will even deliver the beans to your door by bicycle, so if you wanted, you could get your daily caffeine fix without ever leaving the house. But that would be a mistake. Without coming in-store, you'd miss specials like the maple lavender latte.

Picture a coffee shop run by Quentin Tarantino, but instead of all the violence, it's just vibes. That's Pam's Coffy, a funky little café hidden in the Vista Theater (now owned by the director himself). Named after the 1973 film *Coffy*, starring actress Pam Grier, this place is lined with movie posters and filled with colorful, retro chairs. The coffee hails from Jones Coffee Roasters (a brand Tarantino has publicly championed for years).

Cocktail Joints

L.A.'s cocktail scene has always mixed up its own flavors. Sure, you can still find the classics, but how about a nouveau Tiki drink or a seasonal cocktail featuring shrubs from the bartender's backyard?

TIKI-TI

Map 2; 4427 W. Sunset Boulevard, Los Feliz; ///input.monkey.served; www.tiki-ti.com

After years mixing drinks at Hollywood's legendary Polynesian-themed bar Don the Beachcomber, Ray Buhen founded his own spot, Tiki-Ti, in 1961. The crowded dive, now owned by Ray's son and grandson, draws a young, hip crowd for a drink menu that's changed little since its early days. House favorites include Ray's Mistake, which dates back to 1968 and features passion fruit and a dark rum float.

THE ROGER ROOM

Map 3; 370 N. La Cienega Boulevard, Beverly Grove; ///visit.today.toned; www.therogerroom.com

Of course one of L.A.'s finest cocktail bars is right next to the Largo comedy theater – this is the home of show business, after all. Though don't come here expecting any glitz and glamour. The mood at the

Roger Room is more dive-bar chic, with dark lighting and cozy booths. The drinks served here pack a suitably powerful punch – Death in the Afternoon (with absinthe and prosecco) anyone?

HARVARD AND STONE

Map 2; 5221 Hollywood Boulevard, Thai Town; ///deals.frozen.spin; www.harvardandstone.com

Like the speakeasies of old, this dimly lit, vintage-industrial bar feels right at home in grungy-but-cool East Hollywood. It's famed for its top-tier mixology (read: strong drinks), but what really keeps the locals returning again and again are the live rock music acts – and occasional burlesque performances thrown in for good measure.

» **Don't leave without** checking out the backroom bar, which is often taken over by guest bartenders with seasonal cocktail menus.

GOOD TIMES AT DAVEY WAYNE'S

Map 3; 1611 N. El Centro Avenue, Hollywood; ///saving.sock.gazed; goodtimesatdaveywaynes.com

Bored of generic nights out? So are the Houston brothers. They're shaking up L.A. with their epic speakeasies and have truly outdone themselves with Davey Wayne's (named after their dad). Step inside a replica of the family garage, open the refrigerator door, and enter a retro haven full of laid-back 1970s charm. Lounge chairs overflow with cool 20-somethings, while friendly mixologists whip up tasty concoctions like the Fat Elvis (peanut-infused rye whiskey, blackberry shrub, and creme de cacao). Dad would approve.

Solo, Pair, Crowd

Speakeasies are an obvious fit for a city famed for its storytelling – no wonder L.A. has one to suit every mood.

FLYING SOLO

Top-notch cocktails

Craving cocktails but not company? Saddle up to the bar at Lock & Key. The staff at this cozy spot are always up for a chat, and the drinks (made using fresh juices and house-made syrups) are some of the best in town.

IN A PAIR

Eighties vibes

The Slipper Clutch sets an upbeat mood with its 1980s-inspired setting and colorful lights. It's a fun spot for catching up with a pal – and enjoying a bit of friendly competition on the pinball machines.

FOR A CROWD

Bring the band together

Hidden down a secret entrance in Koreatown's Line Hotel, Break Room 86 always promises a fun-filled night. Part-speakeasy, part-karaoke bar, it's the perfect place to bring the gang for a singalong.

THE PRINCE

Map 2; 3198 1/2 W. 7th Street, Koreatown; ///steps.dock.filled; (213) 389-1586

Ever wished your life was more like a sitcom? Grab a drink at the bar where Nick Miller (Jake Johnson) worked in *New Girl*. Part restaurant, part bar, this neighborhood fave is as loved for its Korean fried chicken as it is for its craft cocktails.

BLIND BARBER

Map 6; 5715 N. Figueroa Street, Highland Park; ///guess.finishing.spaces; blindbarber.com

Unlike most of the city's speakeasies, the facade at Blind Barber is actually a functioning business – if you arrive before 8p.m., you can sit down for a trim. In the evenings, it's all about the hidden bar out back, where dates meet for an intimate after-work sip.

» **Don't leave without** trying a delicious Hot Heather, featuring tequila, grapefruit, pineapple, lime, and ginger.

DEATH & CO LA

Map 1; 818 E. 3rd Street, Arts District; ///worth.music.brain; www.deathandcompany.com

Pull up a barstool for a lesson in expert mixology – this West Coast outpost of the famed New York City bar can offer you a cocktail for every mood. Bad audition? Drown your sorrows with a rum-heavy Banned in D.C. Closed a major deal? Celebrate with a whisky-based Queen of the Rodeo. Using local, seasonal ingredients, the bartenders take the art of cocktail making to a whole new level.

Terraces and Rooftops

You didn't come to L.A. to drink inside. Sit at any of these expansive outdoor dining areas, your favorite cocktail in hand, and take in the city's year-round sunshine and stellar views.

GRANDMASTER ROOFTOP

Map 3; 1518 North Cahuenga Boulevard, Hollywood; ///sound.force.motion; grandmasterrecorders.com

With its music history (it's housed atop the former studio of Grandmaster Recorders), sweeping views of the Hollywood Hills, and super-chill clientele, Grandmaster is the epitome of rooftop cool. Come with a pal and kick back over a musically inspired cocktail.

E.P. AND L.P.

Map 3; 603 N. La Cienega Boulevard, West Hollywood; ///gave.crest.mops; www.eplosangeles.com

Looking for a stereotypical social media-ready rooftop scene? This West Hollywood bar and restaurant overdelivers, with its nighttime views of the Hollywood Hills that are good enough to rival a postcard. On the buzzing deck you'll find L.A. rich kids sipping specialty cocktails, friends out celebrating birthdays, and stylistas who just want someone to notice their designer sneakers. The only drawback is the difficulty of getting in – there's always a line out the door on weekend nights.

TONY'S ON THE PIER

Map 5; 210 Fisherman's Wharf, Redondo Beach; ///marker.dinner.softly; www.oldtonys.com

Since the 1950s, "Old Tony's" has been offering no-nonsense locals affordable mai tais and panoramic views of the water right on Fisherman's Wharf. The old-school seaside vibe – complete with fishing nets hanging from the ceiling – is perfectly complemented by its charming pier location and classic seafood dishes. (The oysters are some of the freshest you'll find in the South Bay.)

» **Don't leave without** ordering a mai tai. It's so legendary that it even comes in a souvenir glass you get to take home.

HIGH ROOFTOP

Map 4; 1697 Pacific Avenue, Venice; ///glow.flames.cheat; www.hotelerwin.com

Sitting atop the trendy Hotel Erwin, this lively cocktail bar is a great spot to see all of L.A. life on the Venice boardwalk below. Don't be put off by the intimidating bouncers – you'll find everyone feels at home here, whether that's nervous first dates, overdressed tourists, or surfer bros coming in from the waves.

BELMONT BREWING COMPANY

Map 5; 25 39th Place, Long Beach; ///wiser.cheater.dices; www.belmontbrewing.com

Right on the water, this brewpub – the oldest one operating in SoCal – attracts both sun-weathered old-timers and fresh-faced students with pitchers of classic brews. Enjoy miles of oceanfront and city skyline while sipping on award-winning ales.

» **Don't leave without** trying the Long Beach Crude – an easy-drinking stout brewed in honor of the nearby Signal Hill oil field.

TAVERN TOMOKO & LADYFACE BREWERY

Map 6; 29281 Agoura Road, Agoura Hills; ///cracker.pixies.pushed; www.taverntomoko.com

Looking out from this bar's veranda, with its hilly views of Ladyface Mountain, you could almost imagine you're in the south of France. That's what owner Cyrena Nouzille thinks, anyway, and she does her best to complete the fantasy with her wonderful French-style brews.

MARGOT

Map 4; 8820 Washington Boulevard, Suite 301, Culver City; ///blur.grin.lazy; www.margot.la

The crown jewel of the Culver City restaurant revival, this airy rooftop joint has people from both sides of the 10 Freeway scrambling for a reservation. Join the lucky few sipping regional wines and craft cocktails while taking in 360-degree views of the city.

Liked by the locals

"The rooftop bar craze may have kicked off in N.Y.C., but L.A. perfected it. I can't really think of a better city where you can knock back a pisco sour after work while looking down at the ocean waves almost any time of the year."

ANDREA LEE, SOCIAL MEDIA MANAGER AND SKINCARE INFLUENCER

Wine Bars

With California's wine country just up the coast, it's no surprise that L.A. is full of great wine bars. Whether they're championing rare vintages or eco-friendly newbies, staff will gladly guide you to your perfect sip.

THE RUBY FRUIT

Map 2; 3510 Sunset, Blvd Silver Lake; ///glare.desk.class; www.therubyfruit.com

Named after Rita Mae Brown's coming-of-age classic *Rubyfruit Jungle*, this natural wine bar is one of L.A.'s favorite sapphic spaces. It's beloved by the community for its extensive wine menu and buzzy calendar of events – come for coworking sessions, meetups with women working in film, or literary salons. Even better, for that happy hour that lasts all day on Mondays.

TABULA RASA BAR

Map 2; 5125 Hollywood Boulevard, Thai Town; ///among.coins.glue; www.tabularasabar.com

A Thai Town hangout with an excellent selection of natural wines, Tabula Rasa is one of the best wine bars on this side of the city – though it's so laid-back, you wouldn't know it. The vibe

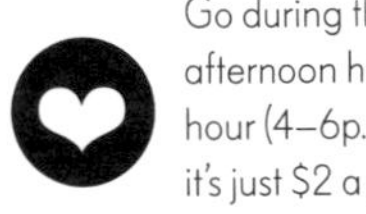
Go during the late afternoon happy hour (4–6p.m.) when it's just $2 a glass for all wines.

here is ultra-chilled, with a low-key industrial aesthetic, mellow mood lighting, and the easy beats of old-school hip-hop in the background.

SALA COFFEE AND WINE

Map 5; 3853 Atlantic Avenue, Long Beach; ///with.wisdom.grills; (562) 269-0476

Coffee and wine: two beverages dear to the heart of many an Angeleno. And Sala does both exceptionally. Call by in the morning for a caffeinated pick-me-up, then return in the afternoon to lazily linger over a bottle of red. The welcoming staff are always open to questions – they love to rave about their wine picks as much as the young, largely Latinx clientele loves to drink them.

» Don't leave without ordering a light bite from whichever friend of the owner's is taking over the kitchen that day.

HI-LO

Map 4; 8582 Washington Boulevard, Culver City; ///paths.lifted.remote; www.hiloliquor.com

More than your friendly neighborhood liquor store, this spot has a special, boutique feel. Part wine shop, part tasting room, it offers hard-to-find wine and beer, charming staff who know the liquor industry from top to bottom, and a gorgeous, well-curated space (plus fun bodega snacks like popped water lily seeds). The best part? As the name suggests, you'll find great pours whatever your budget.

BAR BANDINI

Map 1; 2150 W. Sunset Boulevard, Echo Park; ///rungs.page.linen; www.barbandini.com

Don't let Echo Park's hipsters know we've told you about Bar Bandini – they want to keep this local gem all to themselves. And who can blame them? Chic but relaxed, it's an intimate place that's just as good for trying to impress a date as it is for a hangout with your best friends. The rotating selection of wines is perfectly on trend (read: natural and organic), and if you ask politely they'll even let you sample a few before pouring a glass. Oh, and they also have a pretty good beer selection, too.

ESTERS WINE SHOP & BAR

Map 4; 1314 7th Street, Santa Monica; ///rainy.spice.epic; www.esterswineshop.com

Tucked away from Santa Monica's main street in an elegantly restored Art Deco building, this upscale space – with its cushy lounge seating and see-and-be-seen patio – is the domain of the neighborhood's

Try it!

TRAIN YOUR TASTE BUDS

Learn the art of being a sommelier with Sunday tastings at Esters Wine Shop & Bar. You'll get a themed tasting from the 250-plus selection, curated by in-house expert Randall Elliot.

rich and fashionable. Yes, it's spendy, but who doesn't enjoy a bit of glamour every once in a while? Treat yourself: order a full bottle and some plates of charcuterie (we highly recommend the smoky dates and lavender almonds).

A.O.C.

Map 3; 8700 W. 3rd Street, West Hollywood; ///strike.patch.salt; www.aocwinebar.com

Walking into this warmly lit restaurant and bar, with ivy crawling up the tiled walls, you might think you've left L.A. and arrived at a lush Spanish villa. Founded by a SoCal sommelier duo, this West 3rd Street location has an iconic wine list that pairs beautifully with its Mediterranean-style small plates. If you're on a date, be sure to ask for seating on the romantic, fairy-tale patio.

» **Don't leave without** ordering the Spanish fried chicken – it makes a great accompaniment to a bottle of chardonnay.

MELODY

Map 2; 751 N. Virgil Avenue, East Hollywood; ///quiz.papers.urban; www.melodyla.com

With a bright turquoise front and electric-blue neon trim, this energetic neighborhood wine joint is difficult to miss. Inside, you'll find lively groups of friends drinking generous pours and snacking on creative food from rotating pop-ups. The overall feel is like being at a dinner party, where the drinks and conversation flow so easily you don't realize you've been sitting there for hours.

An evening of cocktails in classic Hollywood

Ah, Hollywood, the birthplace of the movie business. Back in the golden age of cinema, in the 1930s, Tinseltown was dominated by five movie studios and produced 600 films every year. By the middle of the century, however, low theater admissions and censorship rulings meant the industry dwindled, with all but one studio closing. The neighborhood was revitalized in the 80s and regained its popularity – this time for nightlife. A place where tumbledown dives sit next to sexy speakeasies, Hollywood is known for its blend of glamour and grit. So make like you're a star of the silver screen and swig a cocktail in style.

1. Frolic Room
6245 Hollywood Blvd;
(323) 462-5890
///event.trail.excuse

2. Musso and Frank
6667 Hollywood Blvd;
www.mussoandfrank.com
///breath.energy.actor

3. No Vacancy
1727 N. Hudson Ave;
www.novacancyla.com
///cuts.valley.images

4. The Spare Room
7000 Hollywood Blvd; www.spareroomhollywood.com
///critic.woes.depend

Dolby Theatre®
///feeds.bounty.deal

HOLLYWOO
HEIGHTS

FRANKLIN AVENU

Have a ball at THE SPARE ROOM

End the night with a game of bowling at this cocktail lounge inside the Hollywood Roosevelt Hotel. It was cofounded in 1927 by then-MGM honcho Louis B. Mayer and silent film stars Mary Pickford and Douglas Fairbanks.

0 meters 400
0 yards 400

NORTH HOLLYWOOD CAHUENGA FREEWAY

HIGHLAND AVENUE

BLVD

HOLLYWOOD DELL

The **Dolby Theatre®** *has hosted the annual Academy Awards ceremony since opening in 2001, when the 74th Awards were presented.*

FRANKLIN AVENUE

Imbibe and pretend at
NO VACANCY

This perennial hot spot doesn't actually date back to Hollywood's golden age. You wouldn't know it, though, thanks to actors helping set the vintage scene as you enjoy period-appropriate cocktails.

3

OLLYWOOD BOULEVARD

2

HOLLYWOOD BOULEVARD

1

Turn back the clock at
MUSSO AND FRANK

Hollywood's oldest restaurant, which first opened in 1919, has always had a never-ending list of famous fans, from Marilyn Monroe to Harrison Ford. Ask for one of the famous martinis.

HOLLYWOOD

Dive in at
FROLIC ROOM

Next door to the historic Pantages Theatre, this low-key bar started life as a speakeasy in 1930 before attracting the likes of Judy Garland and Frank Sinatra. Order a cheap drink, sit back, and enjoy people-watching.

EST SUNSET BOULEVARD

WEST SUNSET BOULEVARD

HIGHLAND AVENUE

VINE STREET

FOUNTAIN AVENUE

FOUNTAIN AVENUE

SHOP

The L.A. look is a perfectly styled blend of modern design and one-off vintage finds. From clothes to books to produce, it's all about keeping it cool and local.

Street Style

One of the world's newer fashion headquarters, L.A. is home to an effortlessly cool street style that's still accessible to all. Think casual but high-end: a pair of fresh sneakers, comfy jeans, and your smartest tee.

WEST WEAR

Map 5; 6207 Pacific Boulevard, Huntington Park; ///feels.thank.costs; westwear.us

L.A. wasn't always a hard-core sports town, but ever since the Dodgers (baseball), Lakers (basketball), and Rams (football) became national champions, Angelenos are required to rep gear supporting at least one of the three. Pick your favorite and make your way to unassuming West Wear, where sports fans shop for budget-friendly deals. It's got

Try it!
GO TO A GAME

Now you've got the gear from West Wear, why not show it off at an actual game *(p172)*? Catch a fixture at Dodgers Stadium, watch the Lakers at the Crypto.com Arena, or cheer on the Rams at the SoFi Stadium.

a floor-to-ceiling selection of sports and lifestyle apparel, ready to supply you with all of the hats, socks, and jerseys you could ever possibly want. Go team!

WILD STYLE LA

Map 3; 7703 Melrose Avenue, Melrose; ///thick.crate.brand; wildstylela.com

Want to know what the next big trend will be? Head over to Wild Style. Founded by Tim Hirota (the creative genius behind premium streetwear label Joyrich), the sprawling store showcases the future of street fashion, one up-and-coming designer at a time. It's a favorite with the rich and famous, who are as desperate as anyone else here to be ahead of the curve.

» **Don't leave without** walking across the street to the Joyrich boutique to see what kind of "wearable art" is being sold this season.

DECADES

Map 3; 8214 Melrose Avenue, Melrose; ///crash.corner.tiles; decadesinc.com

There are plenty of places in L.A. to buy vintage fashion, but there's only one Cameron Silver and only one Decades. Known as the "Duke of Melrose," Silver trawls through estate sales (and the closets of celebrities and socialites) before selling his finds at this perfectly curated consignment store. His knack for amassing one-of-a-kind pieces is the envy of the city's wardrobe stylists and deal-hunting fashionistas, who pilgrimage here for secondhand designer gems.

REFORMATION

Map 3; 8000 Melrose Avenue, Beverly Grove; ///shades.quench.sage; www.thereformation.com

If you don't think eco-friendly womenswear can be sexy, then you've never seen someone in a Reformation dress. The cute, sustainable pieces fall somewhere between your classic high street fashion and the haute couture of Rodeo Drive, attracting cult followers in droves. Check out the Ref vintage store down the road, too.

THE HUNDREDS

Map 3; 501 N. Fairfax Avenue, Fairfax; ///spare.major.form; www.thehundreds.com

The staff here may have a reputation for high snobbery, but that doesn't deter all the skaters, hip-hop heads, and cool kids found browsing in the showroom. The Hundreds is, after all, one of L.A.'s

Yes, you can order clothes from Galerie.L.A. online *(www.galerie.la)*, but it's much more fun to make an appointment and shop in real life at the Long Beach showroom. That way, you can talk to Dechel Mckillian, the company's enthusiastic founder and eco-brand evangelist (she's also a celebrity stylist). Her aim is to curate items that match her customers' values, so you'll find garments arranged by categories like BIPOC-owned, ethical production, and vegan.

most iconic streetwear brands, its graphic tees becoming something of a local uniform. Look carefully and you'll spy its exploding cartoon "Adam Bomb" logo all over town.

» **Don't leave without** admiring the giant mastodon skeleton sculpture breaking through the shop's floor.

BIG BUD PRESS

Map 6; 5028 York Boulevard, Highland Park; ///memory.tides.estate; bigbudpress.com

Go bold or go home could easily be the mantra for this colorful store. Specializing in unisex wear, Big Bud Press is beloved for its everyday pieces that come in a range of vibrant hues (with new colors dropping on the regular, much to the delight of L.A.'s art crowd). Tees, jackets, jeans, and work pants form the core range, but it's the unisex jumpsuits that really put this place on the map.

RIPNDIP

Map 3; 441 Fairfax Avenue, Fairfax; ///proof.smashes.leader; www.ripndip.com

Who, we hear you ask, is that mischievous kitty you keep seeing around? You know, the one peeking out of a T-shirt pocket or painted on a wall – with the *Mona Lisa* smile and middle finger crudely raised? This, friends, is Lord Nermal: the viral star of RipNDip. A tongue-in-cheek brand born out of skate culture, RipNDip sells tees, hoodies, and skateboard decks from this gleaming white-walled flagship. It's a super-cool space that's as edgy as his lordship.

Swap Meets and Flea Markets

Malls, schmalls. The real retail heart of Los Angeles is its swap meets and flea markets, where vendors set up rows of stalls and shoppers descend to buy, well, anything and everything.

ALAMEDA SWAP MEET

Map 5; 4501 S. Alameda Street, Central-Alameda; ///cable.rice.noise

Make sure you're wearing comfy shoes – exploring the Alameda Swap Meet is a full-day affair. Spread over several city blocks, this huge indoor bazaar offers every item and service imaginable. Where else can you buy a birthday gift, stock up on cleaning supplies, enjoy a foot massage, grab a taco, and get your taxes done in one go?

SANTA FE SPRINGS SWAP MEET

Map 6; 13963 Alondra Boulevard, Santa Fe Springs; ///opinion.energetic.cars; http://sfsswapmeet.com

"Come for the bargains . . . stay for the fun." So says the Santa Fe Springs slogan, and we couldn't have put it much better ourselves. Part marketplace, part concert venue, it's got the lively buzz of a town square. Families browse for discount car parts and children's toys, while a youthful crowd make a beeline for the food and entertainment (weekends feature an eclectic mix of cover bands and Latin sounds). It's not often you'll find a swap meet open for afternoon and evening shopping, so make the most of it.

LONG BEACH ANTIQUE MARKET

Map 5; 4901 E. Conant Street, Long Beach; ///decreased.expect.scouted; www.longbeachantiquemarket.com

Looking to accessorize your place with a super-stylish vintage coffee-table book? Or how about an exquisitely restored Eames chair? Perhaps an old tin sign, too? You'll find all these and more at Long Beach Antique Market, a veritable homewares heaven. Held on the third Sunday of every month, it offers style from the past at bargain prices.

» Don't leave without buying something decorative for the house – an old freeway sign, say, or a set of 1950s shot glasses.

ROSE BOWL FLEA MARKET

Map 6; 1000 Rose Bowl Drive, Pasadena; ///fully.fancy.ships; www.rgcshows.com/rose-bowl

The $12 admission to this monthly "Flea Market of the Stars" might seem steep, but can you really put a price on easy access to 2,500 of the country's top pop-up vintage and thrift stores? We don't think so. And neither do the Silver Lake hipsters and industry designers who flock here monthly, all desperate to find their next treasure.

L.A. CITY COLLEGE SWAP MEET

Map 2; 4133 Marathon Street, East Hollywood; ///weedy.battle.looked; laccswap.com

Okay, to be fair, the "LACC Swap" is more like a large weekend garage sale than a true swap meet (where you'd find a labyrinth of market stalls). But for only $1 admission, you can join East Hollywood's Central American community as they scour the stalls for clothing, housewares, and produce. If you can't decide whether to splash out on that vintage Dodgers tee, just remember that one-third of the meet's sales revenue goes toward scholarships at L.A. City College – so you're not just treating yourself; you're giving back to the neighborhood, too.

PARAMOUNT SWAP MEET

Map 5; 7900 All America City Way, Paramount; ///song.agents.lift; www.paramountswap.com

Breaking up the South L.A. sprawl, Paramount is a daily swap meet with acres upon acres of rock-bottom-priced goods. Why, yes, that is an entire table of untouched insulated tumblers for $3 each. And did you see the rows of discount gold and silver jewelry? What about all the tag-on lingerie and socks being sold for pennies on the dollar? Even if you're not running low on homewares and undergarments, the deals here are too good to resist. Show up with a $20 bill and go home happy.

» **Don't leave without** getting a *michelada* (a Mexican cocktail featuring beer, spicy tomato juice, and lime) – it's the perfect way to quench your thirst as you wander the aisles.

Liked by the locals

"The swap meet is mythic in Los Angeles – it's so much more than an affordable place to shop. Swap meets are where neighborhoods create community, reaffirm identity, and build collective memories."

SAMANTA HELOU HERNANDEZ,
BILINGUAL MULTIMEDIA JOURNALIST

Home Touches

L.A. living means bright, airy spaces, artistic accents, and a constant push and pull between minimalist modern and maximalist quirk. Decorate your space with a bit of city style from these local favorites.

ROLLING GREENS

Map 4; 9528 Jefferson Boulevard, Culver City; ///areas.admiral.ramp; https://rghomeandgarden.com

Looking to up your greenery game? Pay a visit to Rolling Greens' Culver City flagship. Its design experts will help you get your home garden looking social media-ready in no time. And even if you're not all that into plants (yet), this seasonal nursery is worth a trip just to stroll around the terraced grounds. Wind your way through

Try it!

STYLE UP YOUR PLANTS

Take a hands-on class or workshop at the Rolling Greens "Arrangement Bar," where plant experts will teach you how to make wreaths, succulents, and potted plants good enough for a movie set.

blooming greenhouses, nooks filled with vintage furnishings, and an epic collection of suitably stylish containers. It's like stepping into the pages of a glossy design magazine.

HD BUTTERCUP

Map 4; 3225 Helms Avenue, Culver City; ///limes.second.page; https://hdbuttercup.com

If you've ever dreamed of finding an indie homewares store the size of IKEA, try shopping at HD Buttercup. This 150,000-sq-ft (14,000-sq-m) design and furniture emporium is where Angelenos of all ages browse and scheme for their future homes. Classic or modern, vintage or industrial, there's bound to be something that'll suit your style.

CREATURE'S PLANTS AND COFFEE

Map 2, 4958 N. Eagle Rock Boulevard, Eagle Rock; ///clip.apples.leap; creatures-plants-coffee.com

Eagle Rock residents come to this queer-owned, community staple for the plants *and* the coffee – because both are given the attention they deserve. The former are largely contained in a 50-ft- (15-m-) tall greenhouse and run the gamut from indoor tropical plants to drought-tolerant species, including a savvy collection of succulents. As for the coffee, it's made of beans from local roaster UNITY and served alongside a delicious rotation of pastries. Perfection.

» **Don't leave without** asking about upcoming events. Creature's hosts everything from clothes swaps to botanical talks.

GOLD BUG

Map 6; 38 E. Holly Street, Pasadena; ///awake.rods.grid; www.goldbugpasadena.com

It can get a little macabre, what with the insect taxidermy and all, but there's no doubt that Gold Bug is one of L.A.'s most distinctive home goods stores. Secreted down a side alley, with rotating collections of art, jewelry, and offbeat artifacts (think anything from $3,000 amber skulls to $20 hand-poured black candles), this modern curiosity shop is more like a shoppable museum than a boutique. It's a favorite with gift seekers, who know they'll always find something for the friend who has it all – apart from an anatomical heart lamp, of course.

» **Don't leave without** buying a statement piece (of any price), so you can quiz friendly owner Theodora Coleman about the artist who created it.

LEAF AND SPINE

Map 6; 5440 York Boulevard, Highland Park; ///firmly.super.holly; (323) 257-5323

The indoor plant scene in L.A. has gone as wild as a pothos vine without a climbing guide. Seemingly every neighborhood has a store where homeworkers can get some greenery for their office, but only Highland Park has one luring plant parents from across L.A. County (and even from other states). At Leaf and Spine, owner Dustin Bulaon has curated a unique stash of aroids, succulents, and begonias that take the humble houseplant to an all-new level – some of the rare specimens here can cost hundreds of

Keep an eye on social media for the store's "plant drops," when highly sought-after species go on sale.

dollars per pot. It's the best place in town to buy a plant too expensive to kill – giving you a very good incentive to water it.

BERBERE IMPORTS

Map 4; 8728 Aviation Boulevard, Inglewood; ///love.spirit.zeal; berberelmports.com

Imagine the entire Silk Road flowing into a 50,000-sq-ft (4,645-sq-m) L.A. showroom, and you'll have a rough idea of what to expect at Berbere. For more than 40 years, owner Suad Cano has been using her energy and expert negotiation skills to import artisan homewares from Africa, Asia, and the Middle East. These frequent buying trips have resulted in a wonderland of a store that stocks everything from centuries-old pottery to customized Indian doors (and every Balinese Buddha statue in between).

POP UP HOME

Map 2; 642 N. Western Avenue, East Hollywood; ///dusty.move.pipe; www.popuphome.com

This vibey furniture showroom is where L.A.'s design enthusiasts come to dream (and sometimes splurge). Curated by owner Tricia Benitez Beanum, Pop Up Home's covetable and constantly changing inventory oozes laid-back luxury, and locals can't get enough. Be sure to follow the store's Instagram to catch new arrivals (like statement sofas and post-modern light fixtures) before they're snapped up.

Record Stores

As the unofficial capital of the West Coast music scene, L.A. loves its records. Sure, times haven't always been easy for the city's stores, but these survivors are proof that vinyl is here to stay.

RECORD SURPLUS

Map 4; 12436 Santa Monica Boulevard, Sawtelle; ///stews.atoms.mirror; www.recordsurplusla.com

L.A. is full of gutsy risk-takers following their dreams, and Record Surplus is a prime example. In the late 2010s, when many record stores were closing, it took the brave decision to expand. The move paid off, and it's now home to one of the largest selections of new and used vinyl in town. Join deal seekers digging through stacks of jazz, soul, blues, Latin, reggae, country, hip-hop, and more.

THE RECORD PARLOUR

Map 3; 6408 Selma Avenue, Hollywood; ///short.preoccupied.judges; (323) 464-7757

Analog music lovers of the world, unite! This self-described "Emporium of 20th Century Entertainment" is vintage audio heaven – think retro signage, old-school music equipment, and crate upon crate of records. It'll take you back to a time before Spotify, when vinyl was the only way to bring music to your ears, and the local characters browsing the aisles all wore trilbies (here, many still do).

AMOEBA MUSIC

Map 3; 6200 Hollywood Boulevard, Hollywood; ///clock.behind.torn; www.amoeba.com

Cool kids want to work here, rock stars want to play here, and everyone else wants to buy records here: Amoeba Music is a true West Coast icon. Jam-packed with all the CDs, vinyl, and merch your heart could ever desire, this Hollywood store is truly huge – in fact, it's so big you need a map to navigate around. Block out an afternoon, or even a whole day, for some serious rummaging.

» **Don't leave without** seeing an in-store performance. It's an honor for major musical acts to play the Amoeba stage while in L.A.

FREAKBEAT RECORDS

Map 6; 13616 Ventura Boulevard, Sherman Oaks; ///starts.flank.remark; www.freakbeatrecords.com

Quality over quantity sums up the record store scene in the San Fernando Valley – and Freakbeat leads the (small) pack. The staff here are knowledgeable music nerds who've curated a flawless selection of records, ranging across all genres, from folk to funk. Okay, you might not always find the latest big-name release here, but you'll always discover something fun and new.

FINGERPRINTS MUSIC

Map 5; 420 E. 4th Street, Long Beach; ///provide.central.stud; www.fingerprintsmusic.com

Fingerprints casts off the classic grungy, dusty record store feel in favor of a more laid-back look: think high ceilings, exposed brick, industrial lighting, and a super-cool collection of poster art. But that's not to say it's all style over substance: the vinyl collection here is just as well curated as the decor. Rock, rap, jazz, hip-hop – you name it, Fingerprints has got it. Want to get your hands on something extra special? Time your visit here with Record Store Day. Fingerprints is the local HQ for events, and it's always got the latest exclusives.

» **Don't leave without** enjoying a latte or a nutritious lunch on the streetside patio at Berlin, the coffee shop and all-day bistro that stands next door.

ROCKAWAY RECORDS

Map 2; 2395 Glendale Boulevard, Silver Lake; ///poem.allow.sparks; www.rockaway.com

This one's for all the die-hard collectors out there. Rockaway's owners, Greg and Wayne Johnson, have spent more than 40 years buying up the vinyl collections of label execs, studio engineers, and DJs, whose unwanted goods are music fan gold. Part museum, part record store (note: you'll need to make an appointment to visit), Rockaway has got enough rare vinyl, posters, gold records, instruments, and backstage passes to make even the most experienced crate diggers totally lose their cool. Always wanted a still-sealed copy of The Beatles' iconic *White Album*? How about an original *The Velvet Underground & Nico* LP, complete with banana sticker? Well, now's your chance. Heck, why not throw in a 1984 Van Halen tour tee while you're at it?

PERMANENT RECORDS

Map 2; 1906 Cypress Avenue, Cypress Park; ///salad.served.count; www.permanentrecordsla.com

Permanent's curatorial philosophy is "all killer no filler," and it's fair to say it delivers just that. Not only does the store sell a tantalizing selection of vintage rock vinyl and obscure punk releases, but it also makes music; the store has its own independent label, putting out limited releases from local artists. And, on top of that, it has its own bar, the Roadhouse. While away a couple of hours here, rubbing shoulders with Highland Park's vintage-wearing tastemakers and music-head hipsters, flicking through the stacks of records before settling down with a beer to admire your latest finds.

Try it!
CATCH A SHOW

Why not top off some shopping with a show? At the Permanent Records Roadhouse (next door to the store), you can catch an amateur comedy show or a local band nearly any night of the week.

Book Nooks

L.A. loves a good story, so it's no surprise that the city's bookstores are thriving. If you're in need of a book for a beach day, then these spots have got you (hard)covered.

THE LAST BOOKSTORE

Map 1; 453 S. Spring Street, Downtown; ///mint.bets.wire; www.lastbookstorela.com

In 2015, when John Spencer decided to open a used bookstore in a downtown loft, he assumed that the project would fail due to the decline of the bookselling industry (hence the name). Turns out he was wrong. The Last Bookstore has since expanded into a multistory hub, becoming the largest new and used bookstore

Try it!

GO TO A POETRY SLAM

Enjoy literature brought to life with The Definitive Soapbox, a popular Slam poetry event in Long Beach. Check social media for details of the next event and the annual festival.

in California. Among its labyrinthine aisles, you'll find folks browsing for the latest bestseller, hidden nooks lined with funky artworks, and books that literally fly off the shelves in spectacular sculptural displays. How could it not have been doomed for success?

» Don't leave without checking out the expansive and very rad vinyl record collection on the main floor. You can't miss it.

SKYLIGHT BOOKS

Map 2; 1818 N. Vermont Avenue, Los Feliz; ///hurt.good.mice; www.skylightbooks.com

This light and airy space – complete with a leafy ficus tree in the middle – is a literary pillar of the artsy Los Feliz neighborhood. It's a great place to meet other book lovers, whether that's by getting a recommendation from the welcoming staff or making a new friend at a live reading. Oh, look out for Fanny, the bookstore cat, often found curled up in one of the cozy armchairs.

RE/ARTE CENTRO LITERARIO

Map 1; 2014 1/2 E. Cesar E. Chavez Avenue, Boyle Heights; ///toward.record.amuse; www.reartela.com

Launched by local poet Viva Padilla, this literary and art center grew out of the much-respected South L.A. literary journal *Dryland*. It's got an awesome selection of accessibly priced books by Black and Brown authors, though it's the events that really make this place a bustling community hub. Check out the calendar for a packed program of book readings, open mic nights, and movie screenings.

BOOK SOUP

Map 3; 8818 Sunset Boulevard, West Hollywood; ///video.bleat.bright; www.booksoup.com

Nestled alongside the music venues and nightclubs of the iconic Sunset Strip, Book Soup is as legendary as the rock stars who shop here (Elton John is a loyal customer). A city stalwart since 1975, it's filled with sweeping floor-to-ceiling bookshelves, rare books, a vast magazine section, and limited-edition vinyl. Frequent readings from authors and celebrities only add to the L.A. vibe.

VROMAN'S

Map 6; 695 E. Colorado Boulevard, Pasadena; ///sits.slap.moods; www.vromansbookstore.com

Vroman's might be one of the oldest bookstores in Southern California (it was founded in 1894), but it's still got a youthful buzz. In fact, it's super child-friendly, with teen book clubs and kids' storytime, making it a great place to visit with young ones in tow. And the best bit? There's an in-store wine bar. Kick back with a glass and a new page-turner while the kids are being entertained.

REPARATIONS CLUB

Map 4; 3054 S. Victoria Avenue, West Adams; ///awake.dame.fines; rep.club

With its photo-ready book displays, colorful couches, and jazz soundtrack, Rep Club is the kind of place you'll stay much longer than expected. This intimate bookstore (which champions Black authors) is like a home from home, with staff welcoming you as part of the family. Even online orders come with a sweet, handwritten thank-you note.

THE RIPPED BODICE

Map 4; 3806 Main Street, Culver City; ///sharp.live.activism; www.therippedbodicela.com

Lover of love? A trip to this indie bookstore is a must. Housed in Culver City behind an unabashedly pink storefront, the suggestively named Ripped Bodice was launched by two sisters, eager to create a feminist and sex-positive space where readers could browse steamy erotica without being judged. They succeeded: pick up a tome and enjoy a raunchy read with pride.

» Don't leave without signing up for the "Read, Romance, Repeat" subscription box, which sends a titillating book to your door every month.

TÍA CHUCHA'S CENTRO CULTURAL & BOOKSTORE

Map 6; 12677 Glenoaks Boulevard, Sylmar; ///ages.onion.pencil; www.tiachucha.org

When this store first opened in 2001, the northeast San Fernando Valley had no bookstores, art galleries, or major cultural spaces. Now, thanks to Tía Chucha's, the community not only has somewhere to buy culturally diverse books but also a thriving program of workshops and events (in both Spanish and English) to attend. A whole new creative scene from one little bookstore – not bad, eh?

Farmers' Markets

With much of the nation's food supply coming from California, it makes sense that farmers' markets are a big thing in L.A. While most are hyperlocal, here's a few that have become destinations in themselves.

MAR VISTA FARMERS' MARKET

Map 4; Venice Boulevard at Grand View Street, Mar Vista; ///status.wire.clip; www.marvistafarmersmarket.org

Set your alarm and get to this Sunday street fair early; it's the only way you're guaranteed to snag a table in the dining section. Mar Vista might look like any other modest neighborhood farmers' market, but, in fact, it's home to some of the county's most imaginative pop-up food vendors. Prepare to jostle with yogis and tech workers at stalls serving tasty plates of things like barbecue and vegan soul food.

SANTA MONICA FARMERS' MARKET

Map 4; Arizona Avenue, between 2nd and 4th streets, Santa Monica; ///wool.motor.calls; www.santamonica.gov

The granddaddy of L.A. farmers' markets, this weekly multi-block behemoth has been the place to get fresh produce since way before it was cool (read: this is the market that made it cool). Every

Wednesday morning, famous chefs and health-conscious Westsiders descend for the latest hauls of SoCal's finest fruits and vegetables. It's a feast of freshness, so make sure you bring an appetite.

» Don't leave without **visiting the Weiser Farms stall, a family-owned operation that sells vegetables to many of L.A.'s top restaurants.**

GRAND CENTRAL MARKET

Map 1; 317 S. Broadway, Downtown; ///casino.served.trader; www.grandcentralmarket.com

L.A. is constantly reinventing itself, and Grand Central Market is no exception. One of the fanciest markets on the West Coast when it opened in 1917, it later became known as a cheap spot to pick up some produce or a grab-and-go lunch. Nowadays, it's on its third incarnation as a lively destination for chef-driven food (shout out to Eggslut, Sticky Rice, and Sarita's Pupuseria), forever bustling with hungry foodies. Who knows where it will take things next.

LONG BEACH SOUTHEAST CERTIFIED FARMERS' MARKET

Map 5; 2nd Street and N. Marina Drive, Long Beach; ///whips.collects.city; www.goodveg.org/sunday-long-beach-southeast

Shopping in the sun is always a treat, but it's even better with the waft of a cool sea breeze. This oceanside Sunday pop-up – "The Marina Market" to regulars – is the perfect place to browse without working up a sweat. Pro tip: grab some baked goods and fresh fruit and picnic at the nearby marina, overlooking the splashy boats.

THE ORIGINAL FARMERS' MARKET

Map 3; 6333 W. 3rd Street, Fairfax; ///scarcely.chops.pull; www.farmersmarketla.com

First a place for farmers to sell produce from their trucks, this L.A. staple has grown into a maze of built-in stalls hawking everything from fresh pastries to meat to ice cream. The best bit? It's permanent, so you can shop here seven days a week.

» **Don't leave without** buying a hot lunch at one of the food counters. Our pick is the Gumbo Pot, serving a mix of Cajun specialties.

STUDIO CITY FARMERS' MARKET

Map 6; Ventura Place, Studio City; ///remind.played.steer; www.studiocityfarmersmarket.com

Meeting friends with kids? Head to this Sunday San Fernando Valley farmers' market. Little ones are kept busy by the play area, climbing wall, and bounce house, so you'll be able to, you know, actually make purchases without all their adorable distractions.

HOLLYWOOD FARMERS' MARKET

Map 3; Selma and Ivar, Hollywood; ///nest.renew.kinds; www.seela.org/markets-hollywood

Think Hollywood and the tourist trap that is the Walk of Fame probably comes to mind. Beyond that, though, is a flourishing community with some pockets of serious cool – like this Sunday pop-up. It features produce stalls and funky artisans like Marianne's Clay Creations, as well as one-of-a-kind food vendors like Marcie's Pies. Yum.

Liked by the locals

"More than anywhere else, the farmers' markets in L.A. really highlight ingredients at the peak of their season. There's always something unique and exciting to play with, things you've never heard of, like apriums – that's apricot plus plum."

MELISSA ORTIZ,
EXECUTIVE CHEF, ROSE PARK ON PINE

LONG BEACH

EAST 7TH STREET

CHERRY AVENUE

JUNIPERO AVENUE

EAST 6TH STREET

Dig for treasure at
ASSISTANCE LEAGUE THRIFT STORE

It's hard to resist this volunteer-run thrift store, which bursts at the seams with carefully curated clothing and home goods at affordable prices.

Coast into
PIGEON'S ROLLER SKATE SHOP

Nowhere celebrates SoCal's roller-skate scene like this one-stop shop. Make like it's the 90s and get fitted for a colorful pair of quads by experts from the local derby scene.

1 2 3 4

EAST 4TH STREET

Shop sustainably at
FAR OUTFIT

While this vintage clothing store is packed with cool clothes, it's also beloved among locals for its selection of sustainable gifts.

Go crate-digging at
THIRD EYE RECORDS

For the record: Third Eye is *the* place to go for preloved vinyl. Chat to owner Gary, who is only too happy to recommend a band or artist.

CHERRY AVENUE

JUNIPERO AVENUE

WISCONSIN AVENUE

EAST 3RD STREET

LONG BEACH

0 meters 200

0 yards 200

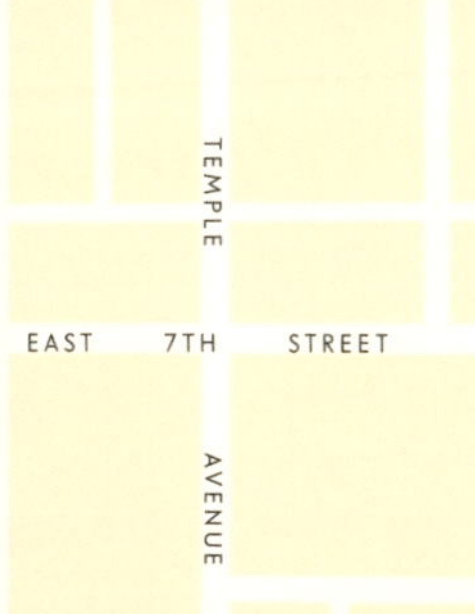

A morning shopping on
Retro Row

Angelenos have been shopping for vintage fashion long before it was cool. And their thrifting go-to? That's 4th Street in Long Beach, also known as Retro Row, thanks to the slew of kitsch vintage stores that opened here in the 1990s. Today, this homey street is lined with locally owned independent shops and boutiques, as well as retro stores, of course. Grab a tote and take a morning stroll down this well-trodden street, stocking up on goodies for your home and closet.

Pick up a rad read at PAGE AGAINST THE MACHINE

Dip into one of Long Beach's newer independent bookstores, a punny ode to the owner's proclivity for radical reads, zines, and alternative thinking.

5

Baker Arturo Enciso used to sell all manner of bread and pastries from his living room before opening **Gusto Bread** *in August 2020.*

TEMPLE

EAST 3RD STREET

AVENUE

1. Far Outfit
2020 E. 4th St, Long Beach; faroutfit.com
///issue.shorten.snoring

2. Assistance League Thrift Store
2100 E. 4th Street; www.assistanceleague.org/long-beach
///panics.drum.sheets

3. Pigeon's Roller Skate Shop
2148 E. 4th Street; www.pigeonskates.com
///using.massing.however

4. Third Eye Records
2234 E. 4th Street; www.thirdeyerecordshop.com
///doctors.breath.snuggle

5. Page Against the Machine
2714 E. 4th Street; www.patmbooks.com
///user.hesitate.froze

Gusto Bread
///crystal.servants.stored

ARTS & CULTURE

Lights, camera, action! L.A. is, of course, the home of movie magic, but it also has a diverse cultural scene that ranges from quirky museums to thought-provoking art.

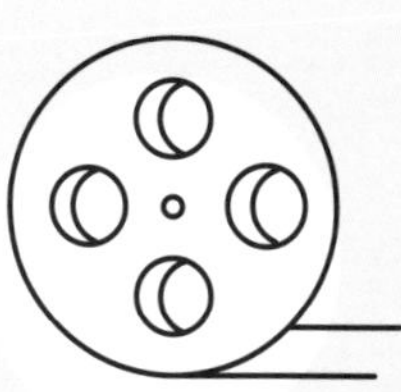

City History

Throughout L.A.'s short history, countless communities and movements have found a home here, resulting in a rich past (and present) that's represented at these important spots.

RANCHO LOS ALAMITOS

Map 5; 6400 E. Bixby Hill Road, Long Beach; ///version.unrealistic.rapport; www.rancholosalamitos.com

Farming probably isn't the first industry you associate with L.A., but in fact it's been part of the city's economy for centuries. At this historic ranch, you can get a taste of 19th-century agricultural life (complete with barnyard animals) – and learn about the Indigenous Tongva-Gabrielino people, who were displaced by the farm's founders.

ONE GALLERY

Map 3; 626 N. Robertson Boulevard, West Hollywood; ///rents.honest.faded; www.onearchives.org

There's more to L.A.'s queer culture than WeHo's famous bars and clubs. Protests against LGBTQ+ discrimination in the city date back to the 1960s, and the queer publication *The Advocate* was founded here in 1967. Today, the city is home to the largest collection of

LGBTQ+ materials in the world – the ONE Archives at the University of Southern California Libraries – which are curated into rotating exhibitions at this partner space. Past topics have ranged from AIDS activism to queer Chicanx artists of the 1960s–90s.

JAPANESE AMERICAN NATIONAL MUSEUM

Map 1; 100 N. Central Avenue, Little Tokyo ///diary.reap.stream; www.janm.org

Founded in 1985, this museum was the brainchild of a group of World War II veterans and Little Tokyo businessmen, eager to preserve the history of Japanese Americans in the city – one of its early exhibitions encouraged locals to share their stories of being forcibly relocated to internment camps during the war. Popular with history buffs, it's also an inspiring space for creative thinkers, with changing exhibits on celebrated artists and topics like Japanese tattoo traditions.

MARIACHI PLAZA

Map 1; 1831 1st Street, Boyle Heights; ///urgent.bills.since

Mexican culture is an integral part of L.A. life – around 30 per cent of the city's population has Mexican ancestry – and it's kept alive and well in Boyle Heights. In a tradition that began in the 1930s, elegant mariachi musicians gather at this square to showcase their talents in the hope of being hired for paying gigs.

» **Don't leave without** getting a meal at Birrieria Don Boni, a casual joint around the corner that specializes in tender birria (stewed goat).

CALIFORNIA AFRICAN AMERICAN MUSEUM (CAAM)

Map 4; 600 State Drive, Exposition Park; ///divisions.deny.advice; https://caamuseum.org

Black people have been shaping Los Angeles from its inception – like Biddy Mason, who got her freedom from enslavement in the early 1850s and went on to become a successful businesswoman in local real estate. Her story is just one of many that's been shared at this fascinating museum, which focuses on Black culture, history, and visual art in California and the West. It's the kind of space best explored with a friend: the exhibits have a knack for being cleverly thought-provoking, and you'll want a buddy to chew them over with.

EL PUEBLO DE LOS ANGELES

Map 1; 125 Paseo de la Plaza, Downtown; ///landed.models.strain; elpueblo.lacity.org

Without the El Pueblo district, there would be no L.A. – it was here that the City of Angels was born, founded in 1781 by Mexican settlers on the land of the Chumash and Tongva peoples. And without Christine Sterling, there wouldn't be the El Pueblo that we know today. A wealthy Californian, she led a campaign in the 1920s to save the area from demolition and also established the "traditional" Mexican marketplace on Olvera Street. Despite being created for Anglo visitors (and glossing over issues of colonization), the area has become a vibrant cultural center for the city's Mexican community.

» **Don't leave without** visiting the Chinese American Museum on N. Los Angeles Street, housed in a building constructed in 1890.

Liked by the locals

"Black culture is thriving in Los Angeles, and CAAM is a critical hub to explore it, presenting work by dynamic artists and scholars in a space that has for decades been dedicated to this vision. I think you sense that history when you enter our galleries."

CAMERON SHAW, EXECUTIVE DIRECTOR AT THE CALIFORNIA AFRICAN AMERICAN MUSEUM

Favorite Museums

Few places celebrate L.A.'s endless creativity better than the city's artsy museums. Ranging from the strange to the sublime, these inventive spaces are our top picks.

MUSEUM OF NEON ART

Map 2; 216 S. Brand Boulevard, Glendale; ///actual.turns.stack; www.neonmona.org

Follow the call of the brightly lit diver atop this museum and plunge into a quirky collection of neon and kinetic pieces. Vintage items trace the history of neon signs (including the use of questionable cultural stereotypes), while contemporary examples showcase the exciting future of this electrifying art (pun firmly intended).

MUSEUM OF JURASSIC TECHNOLOGY

Map 4; 9341 Venice Boulevard, Culver City; ///with.items.puzzle; www.mjt.org

No description can truly capture the magic of this place, which is just as bewildering as its name makes it sound. Inside, you'll discover a mysterious world of dimly lit displays that include "The Lives of Perfect Creatures: Dogs of the Soviet Space Program" and the

Head to the museum's leafy rooftop garden to enjoy some sun while surrounded by chirping birds.

miniature work of Hagop Sandaldjian, which features Disney characters standing on top of needles. It's a bizarre cabinet of curiosities treasured by Angelenos.

CRAFT CONTEMPORARY

Map 3; 5814 Wilshire Boulevard, Mid-Wilshire; ///monday.coats.saves; www.craftcontemporary.org

Can't get the creative juices flowing? Pop to Craft Contemporary for a hit of inspiration. It's always got something new and cool going on – like the time its exterior was covered in 15,000 crochet granny squares by Yarn Bombing Los Angeles. Exhibitions cover all types of innovative craft practices, from ceramics and weaving to video art.

» Don't leave without visiting the gift shop, which offers thoughtfully curated items such as ceramics, books, and textiles.

MUSEUM OF LATIN AMERICAN ART

Map 5; 628 Alamitos Avenue, Long Beach; ///found.official.formally; molaa.org

Fun fact: back in the 1920s, what is now the main entrance area of this museum functioned as a roller-skating rink. The speeding skaters have long gone, but the space lives on for laid-back artsy types who pass lazy afternoons in the galleries here. A few even skip the collection and head straight to the Robert Gumbiner Sculpture & Events Garden – with its bright pink walls and outdoor artworks, it's an ideal place to soak up the sun or doodle in a sketchbook.

Solo, Pair, Crowd

Exploring an epic art collection is always fun with the right company (even if that's just your sketchbook).

FLYING SOLO

Take your time

The largest art museum on the West Coast, the encyclopedic L.A. County Museum of Art (LACMA) is perfect for introspective art lovers who want to explore multiple exhibitions alone with their thoughts.

IN A PAIR

Downtown date

With its casual-yet-cool downtown setting, the Broad Museum is a great date option. Swap life stories as you admire contemporary artworks from household names like Kara Walker and Jeff Koons.

FOR A CROWD

Family-friendly fun

Not only does The Getty have an amazing art collection, but it also has the picturesque Central Garden. This means plenty of outdoor space for kids to roam around – and there's wine on-site for the adults, too.

VINCENT PRICE ART MUSEUM

Map 6; 1301 Avenida Cesar Chavez, Monterey Park; ///gates.detail.happy; vincentpriceartmuseum.org

In a plot twist you might not have seen coming from the name, this isn't a museum filled with artworks by (or of) horror-movie icon Vincent Price. In fact, it gets its moniker because the collection was started by Price and his wife Mary Grant, who donated some of their personal artworks to East Los Angeles College. Now a fully fledged art institution, it draws a diverse mix of antique art lovers (it's famed for its pieces from the Ancient Americas) and cutting-edge creatives checking out the contemporary Latinx art shows.

» Don't leave without exploring work by local artists and makers at the nearby Plaza de la Raza cultural center.

ACADEMY MUSEUM

Map 3; 6067 Wilshire Boulevard, Mid-Wilshire; ///space.outer.gets; www.academymuseum.org

As the home of Hollywood, L.A. is synonymous with the movie industry. It's only fitting, then, that the city is also the location of the country's largest museum on the subject. (And it's a suitably glitzy one, too, with a larger-than-life globe-shaped theater designed by Renzo Piano.) The whole place is a cinephile's dream – the core exhibition, where you can meet the actual E.T.; the exclusive products in the gift shop (like vinyl soundtracks curated by Amoeba Music, *p93*); and the state-of-the-art theaters where you can catch a movie. There's even a chance to experience what it's like to win an Oscar – just make sure you've prepped your acceptance speech.

Public Art

L.A. is a city of spectacle, and its streets and public spaces are no exception. You'll find amazing art in every corner of town, often bringing social commentary as well as color.

WATTS TOWERS

Map 5; 1727 E. 107th Street, Watts; ///successes.basin.orders; www.wattstowers.org

Sometimes, art is simply about the joy of creating. Begun in 1921, this now-iconic installation on a street in Watts was the passion project of Italian American Sabato "Simon" Rodia. For no other reason than the heck of it, he constructed the multicolored towers over the course of three decades. The end result looks like a mini Sagrada Familia, built entirely out of recycled materials.

URBAN LIGHT

Map 3; 5905 Wilshire Boulevard, Mid-Wilshire; ///rocket.army.flats; collections.lacma.org/node/214966

Every major city has a large-scale art installation that's social media gold, and Chris Burden's *Urban Light* is just that for L.A. (Yes that does mean you'll be competing with wannabe influencers for the best view.) It features rows of street lamps gathered from across Southern California, which turn on automatically when the sun sets. The effect is magical, and perfect fodder for twinkly nighttime shots.

» Don't leave without looking closely at the details of each lamp; some include small rosebuds as decoration.

THE GREAT WALL OF LOS ANGELES

Map 6; 12900 Oxnard Street, North Hollywood; ///loud.candy.achieving; planning.lacity.org/blog/great-wall-los-angeles

Not one to shy from a challenge, in 1976 local artist Judy Baca embarked on a project to transform a concrete flood control channel into something vibrant and colorful. With the help of the local community and at-risk youth, what started as a 1,000-ft (300-m) mural has since more than doubled – making it the largest of its kind in the world. Its numerous panels tell the history of California, with a conscious emphasis on marginalized and Indigenous communities.

DESTINATION CRENSHAW

Map 4; 5444 Crenshaw Boulevard; ///angle.legs.shot; destinationcrenshaw.la

Set to be the largest Black art program in the U.S. (with a whopping 100 installations and murals lining Crenshaw Boulevard, the center of L.A.'s Black community), Destination Crenshaw is a vibrant celebration of culture. While the project is yet to be completed, there's already plenty to see and do, from colorful murals by local artists to fun-filled community events (follow the program's Instagram for updates.)

MURAL MILE

Map 6; Van Nuys Boulevard, Pacoima; ///terms.drank.learn; www.muralmile.org

The Walk of Fame isn't the only place you'll find famous faces in the city; this collection of artworks in Pacoima features homages to figures like actor Danny Trejo, activist Assata Shakur, and musician Ritchie Valens. Launched by artist Levi Ponce, who felt there wasn't enough art around the neighborhood, Mural Mile is actually more extensive than the name suggests. It comprises over 50 murals in a 3-mile (5-km) radius, often in places where you might not expect them – like the back of the Pacoima Entrepreneurial Center, where a huge piece by Germs explodes with color and references to Mexican heritage.

AMÉRICA TROPICAL MURAL

Map 1; 125 Paseo de la Plaza, Downtown; ///grabs.player.elite; theamericatropical.org

In 1932, when La Plaza Art Center commissioned Mexican artist David Alfaro Siqueiros to create a public artwork on a "Tropical America" theme, it was expecting a pleasantly idyllic scene. Instead, it got a mural depicting a crucified Indigenous Mexican figure, overtly referencing imperialism and the racist treatment of marginalized groups. Swiftly whitewashed to avoid upsetting tourists at the romanticized Mexican marketplace on Olvera Street, the work was all but forgotten until its rediscovery in the 1960s. Today, you can join artists and political activists in paying tribute to the carefully restored mural and learn more about its controversial past at the América Tropical Interpretive Center.

LONG BEACH WALLS

Map 5; start at 927 Pine Avenue, Long Beach; ///reported.rejects.retire; www.powwowlongbeach.com

For one week every summer, Long Beach hosts the international POW! WOW! street art festival. That's great in itself – there are lots of fun pop-up events – but the best part is the legacy that the festival leaves behind. Fresh murals are added each year, so the whole city is being steadily turned into a walkable (or bikeable) art gallery. Why not get your steps in while doing a self-guided tour? Our favorite stops include the characterful posse of panda bears on Pine Avenue by Woes and Hilda Palafox's colorful beachgoers on Redondo Avenue.

» **Don't leave without** keeping an eye out for utility boxes painted by local artists – they're dotted around the city as part of a local program to decorate traffic signal controller cabinets.

L.A. HISTORY: A MEXICAN PERSPECTIVE

Map 4; Natural History Museum of Los Angeles County, 900 W. Exposition Boulevard, Exposition Park; ///twice.branch.sector; nhm.org

Art has the power to spark tough conversations, and this is one of those pieces that proves it. Censored for its warts-and-all depiction of L.A.'s history – including events like the Zoot Suit Riots, the death of Ruben Salazar during the 1970 National Chicano Moratorium March, and the internment of Japanese communities during World War II – Barbara Carrasco's 1981 mural is now back on display for all to see in the Welcome Center of the Natural History Museum.

Architectural Landmarks

L.A. doesn't have just one building style – everyone from mid-century modernists to Spanish colonial revivalists have come here to build their dreams. These boundary-pushing buildings tell the story of L.A.

HOLLYHOCK HOUSE

Map 2; 4800 Hollywood Boulevard, Vermont; ///leap.villa.vine; www.barnsdall.org/hollyhock-house

The first house Frank Lloyd Wright designed in L.A., Hollyhock House was intended as a home for oil heiress Aline Barnsdall (hollyhock was her favorite flower and is a recurring motif throughout the building).

Try it!
MUSEUM ROW

Go on a DIY architecture tour with a walk along Wilshire Boulevard's Museum Row. The buildings along this mile-long strip range from classical (LACMA) to ultra-modern (Petersen Automotive Museum).

The pair's relationship soured, however, when Wright took too long to complete the over-budget project, and Barnsdall refused to live in it. Instead she donated the hilltop palace to the city, to the delight of the many design lovers found noseying around inside.

UNION STATION

Map 1; 800 N. Alameda Street, Downtown; ///youth.appeal.plus; www.unionstationla.com

As one of the last great railroad stations built in the U.S. (in 1939), Union Station is a celebrated piece of history. The Spanish-style building predates the popularity of cars in Los Angeles (hard to imagine now, we know) and was the first stop for countless folks arriving to live their California Dream.

HERITAGE SQUARE MUSEUM

Map 6; 3800 Homer Street, Montecito Heights; ///error.rental.script; www.heritagesquare.org

Think of this as a collection of Victorian Barbie dreamhouses. Over the past 50 years, eight perfectly preserved Victorian mansions have been rescued from demolition across the city and reassembled in this living time capsule. The pastel-colored houses are lovely, but the real magic happens during the museum's themed events. Join Victorian gaming nights, where locals dress up to play period board games, or catch an outdoor movie screening in the garden.

» **Don't leave without** snapping your next profile picture in front of your dream dollhouse (the pink and green colored one is a favorite).

THE DONUT HOLE

Map 6; 15300 Amar Road, La Puente; ///goal.kettles.beeline; (626) 968-2912

Programmatic architecture – where structures are designed to look like what they sell – has got to be one of L.A.'s most weird-yet-wonderful building styles. There are dozens of donut-shaped donut shops in the city, but this one in the Latinx enclave of La Puente is a fun drive-through variation on the theme. Built in 1968, it's comprised of two 26-ft- (8-m-) wide fiberglass donuts connected by a tunnel, which you drive your car through to pick up your order. It's one of the most photographed bakeries in the U.S., with people coming from far and wide to get snaps for their social media feeds.

» **Don't leave without** treating yourself to some donuts, naturally. We recommend a box of the mini glazed cronuts – they're soft, fluffy, and utterly delicious.

SCHINDLER HOUSE

Map 3; 35 N. Kings Road, West Hollywood; ///blues.fields.crops; makcenter.org/sites/schindler-house

Said to be the first-ever house built in the modernist style, this sprawling commune was designed by Austrian architect Robert Schindler. Intended to house two families, the glass-and-concrete structure was built with no bedrooms or dining rooms, pioneering an open-concept floor plan that was groundbreaking in California architecture when it was erected in the early 1920s. It can be hard to appreciate just how revolutionary this was while touring

Check the online calendar for special events at Schindler House, like art shows and lectures.

the interior today – everyone's doing it now, of course – but that doesn't stop the building from being any less beautiful.

THE GAMBLE HOUSE

Map 6; 4 Westmoreland Place, Pasadena; ///boat.outfit.oasis; gamblehouse.org

Prepare for some serious house envy: this is the custom, exquisitely hand-crafted home of your dreams. Designed by iconic architecture firm Greene & Greene, it deftly combines Japanese and Californian aesthetics, blending teak, maple, and oak surfaces with low-slung roofs reminiscent of pagodas. It's one of the finest examples of Arts and Crafts architecture in the U.S., even making it onto the National Register of Historic Places.

LOS ANGELES CENTRAL LIBRARY

Map 1; 630 W. 5th Street, Downtown; ///stocks.dollar.third; www.lapl.org

Built in the 1920s, this historic library is a veritable Art Deco temple to books and learning – it even comes complete with a colorful, sunburst-tiled pyramid at its crown. Inside, the most striking room is the sumptuous Rotunda, decorated with murals depicting the (extremely romanticized) history of California and a gilded, stained-glass globe known as the Zodiac Chandelier. Because you can never have too much Tinseltown glitz, right?

Movie Theaters

In a city that birthed the film industry as we know it, you better believe that the places showing movies are destinations in themselves. Here, theaters are part art gallery, part performance space, and part town square.

EGYPTIAN THEATRE

Map 3; 6712 Hollywood Boulevard, Hollywood; ///stiff.rewarding.bank; www.americancinematheque.com

Even if you're not likely to be invited to walk a red carpet anytime soon, you can still pretend by buying a ticket for the theater that housed the first-ever Hollywood premiere (black tie is completely optional). Renovated in 2022 by Netflix, this iconic space positively oozes Golden Age glamour, with a signature Egyptian theme that includes four large columns at the front, plus vivid hieroglyphics.

VISTA THEATRE

Map 2; 4473 Sunset Drive, Los Feliz; ///Unity.shape.laser; www.vintagecinemas.com

A vintage movie house that first opened in the 1920s, the Vista has more character than most indie theaters. There's the kitschy décor for one thing, not to mention a colorful past that includes screening

Pause out front to admire an eclectic collection of cement handprints that rivals the Chinese Theatre.

adult offerings until a retool in 1980. Purchased by Quentin Tarantino in 2021, it's now a space for literal film fans, screening movies on celluloid only.

NEW BEVERLY CINEMA

Map 3; 7165 Beverly Boulevard, Fairfax; ///shovels.gentle.couch; thenewbev.com

Even though the surrounding neighborhood has evolved to become a bit pricey, at the New Bev you can enjoy daily double features for just the cost of a single ticket. Quentin Tarantino (yep, him again) famously saved this historic theater when he purchased it in 2007; L.A.'s industry nerds still line up for its bill of B-movie, Old Hollywood, and newer offerings curated by the film-obsessed director.

» Don't leave without catching a midnight screening on a Friday of a movie from Tarantino's personal collection.

CINESPIA AT THE HOLLYWOOD FOREVER CEMETERY

Map 2; 6000 Santa Monica Boulevard; ///draw.crowned.chops; cinespia.org

Watching a film in a cemetery might sound strange, but it makes sense when you're in the final resting place of screen luminaries like Judy Garland and Burt Reynolds. Coming to this summer pop-up is an L.A. rite of passage: bring a bottle of wine, and settle onto the grass alongside eager first-timers and nostaligic old hands.

THE FORD

Map 3; 2580 Cahuenga Boulevard E., Hollywood Hills; ///both.posts.lined; www.theford.com

On the screen in front of you is a beloved classic; all around are the Hollywood Hills; and above you twinkle more stars than you'll ever see on the Walk of Fame. This outdoor venue feels a world away from the city, and yet at the same time it's quintessentially L.A.

ELECTRIC DUSK DRIVE-IN

Map 2; 236 N. Central Avenue, Glendale; ///cones.trunk.paused; www.electricduskdrivein.com

It's true: Angelenos love their cars just as much as their movies. So of course this drive-in is one of the city's most popular screening experiences. Operating year-round, its program has something for everyone, from horror favorites to family-friendly gems.

THE FRIDA CINEMA

Map 6; 305 E. 4th Street, Santa Ana; ///email.runs.pausing; thefridacinema.org

This arthouse destination is one for true cinephiles. Yes, you'll have to cross the Orange Curtain into neighboring Orange County, but the double-screen theater in Santa Ana is a bonafide gem. It's got some of the best indie cinema programming in all of SoCal, including an impressive selection from Latinx filmmakers.

» **Don't leave without** exploring the rest of Santa Ana. This vibrant city is quickly becoming a new art, culture, and nightlife destination.

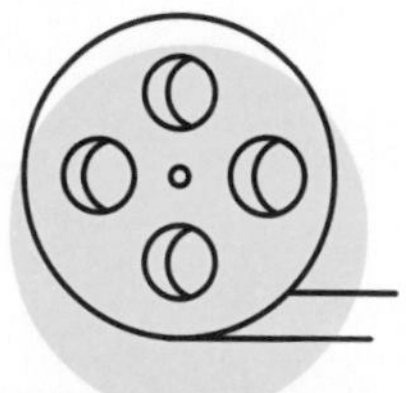

Liked by the locals

"We're a needle in a haystack in terms of arts and culture in Orange County. But I'm very proud of the scene that we have created, basically from scratch."

TREVOR DILLON, PROGRAMMING DIRECTOR AT FRIDA CINEMA

Indie Art Spaces

Angelenos love to express themselves through art, and new talent is emerging here all the time. Check out these intimate art spaces, and you might just discover the next big name.

SELF-HELP GRAPHICS & ART

Map 1; 1300 E. 1st Street, East Los Angeles; ///orange.acute.debate; www.selfhelpgraphics.com

In 1970, four printmakers, frustrated by the lack of facilities for young Chicanx artists, began creating works in an East Los Angeles garage. Fast-forward 50 years, and Self-Help Graphics is now one of the city's most important destinations for Latinx and Chicanx art. Rotating exhibits offer insight into the organization's printmaking

Try it!
TAKE A CLASS

Inspired by the prints you've seen at Self-Help Graphics & Art? Then why not sign up for one of its workshops. Budding artists can try their hand at everything from silkscreen printing to rug weaving.

projects, but this is more than just a gallery space. There's also a long-standing focus on community engagement – its annual Día de los Muertos celebration attracts thousands of Angelenos.

ART + PRACTICE

Map 4; 3401 W. 43rd Place, Leimert Park; ///junior.moment.chains; www.artandpractice.org

Not content with simply being a successful international artist, Mark Bradford is giving back to his childhood community as a founder of Art + Practice. It's a unique nonprofit foundation that supports foster youth, as well as providing this free public art gallery for locals. A welcoming space focusing on artists of color, it makes a great stop on a stroll around the historic Black neighborhood of Leimert Park.

» Don't leave without stopping at nearby café ORA to drink smoothies and snack on tasty salads.

NUCLEUS

Map 6; 210 East Main Street, Alhambra; ///gold.visual.plates; www.gallerynucleus.com

Pop art meets fine art at this playful gallery in Alhambra. Founded in 2004, Nucleus has become (as its name predicted) the beating heart of L.A.'s illustration scene. Aspiring artists flock here for the popular events and networking opportunities, while pop-culture fans stop by to gaze at the regularly changing artwork. You'll find a lot of fantasy-themed paintings, manga artwork, and quirky drawings, most of which are available to purchase (prices start from $100).

SHULAMIT NAZARIAN

Map 3; 616 N. La Brea Avenue, Fairfax; ///manual.crass.senses; www.shulamitnazarian.com

An oasis of calm amid the bustle of Fairfax, Shulamit Nazarian is always showing something cool. On-the-pulse art lovers swing by after brunch, eager to check out the latest mix of paintings, textile pieces, sculptures, and installations. Expect deep themes like immigrant identity and the artist's private self.

RESIDENCY ART GALLERY

Map 4; 1245 District Dr. Suite 945, Inglewood; ///arena.drive.loads; residencyart.com

While many art institutions across L.A. are feeling the pressure to show more artists of color without tokenizing them, spaces like Residency are proving that it's really not all that hard. Local names whose work has appeared here include Texas Isaiah, the first trans

An industrial area of Downtown is probably not the first place you'd expect to find a cutting-edge gallery, yet here the huge Corey Helford Gallery *(https://coreyhelfordgallery.com)* is. It focuses on genres like pop surrealism and graffiti, with pieces that are often bold, intricate, and mischievous. Exhibitions include themed group shows as well as solo showcases for local talent or international names.

photographer to shoot a cover for *Vogue*, and painter Kohshin Finley, whose portraits of his friends and family have an almost photographic quality. The minimal space keeps the focus on the artwork, so you can give it the time and appreciation it deserves.

BAND OF VICES

Map 4; 5351 W. Adams Boulevard, West Adams; ///gather.claps.indoor; www.bandofvices.com

You can't miss the bright pink exterior of this West Adams exhibition space. It's an unapologetic color that chimes perfectly with the gallery's vocal intention to give a platform to historically overlooked creative communities. It's clearly something that people are eager to see more of, as there's now a second Band of Vices space just up the road – this one may have a more muted black façade, but the art inside is no less eye-catching.

HUMAN RESOURCES

Map 1; 410 Cottage Home Street, Chinatown; ///lease.bucks.inform; www.h-r.la

Ready to get conceptual? This not-for-profit space at the corner of a mostly residential block showcases contemporary art that pushes the envelope. On any given day, it could be screening a film, hosting a performance, staging a listening party, or serving as the backdrop for a music video. It's anything but traditional and that's why we love it.

» **Don't leave without** calling at Sesame LA, a charming store selling everything from Asian food essentials to handmade ceramics.

0 meters 400
0 yards 400

Brookside Golf Club *was designed by famed golf architect William P. Bell in the 1920s. The 36-hole course is famed for its incredible views.*

6

Stroll around THE ROSE BOWL

End your tour by exploring the most famous venue in college football history. Designed by architect Myron Hunt, the 1922 structure was inspired by ancient colliseums and can host up to 100,000 fans.

5

Marvel at MILLARD HOUSE

Bookseller Alice Millard commissioned Frank Lloyd Wright to build this house, now known as "La Miniatura." It's very different from his Prairie style, with patterned concrete blocks creating a striking entrance.

4

Stop by the UNITARIAN CHURCH

The American Craftsman porch here is lovely. Take it in before popping into the reflective sanctuary, designed by Pasadena-born Whitney R. Smith in the 1970s.

3

Join a tour at THE GAMBLE HOUSE

Explore the neighborhood's most iconic Greene & Greene house, which is Japanese in style. *Back to the Future* fans will recognize the facade as Doc Brown's house.

2

Sneak a peek at the JAMES A. CULBERTSON HOUSE

Poke your head through the fence of this 1902 gem, built by Arts and Crafts architects Charles and Henry Greene for their loyal client, James A. Culbertson. The English-inspired house draws heavily on the works of designer William Morris.

1

Start at the MYRON HUNT RESIDENCE

Scope out the house of Rose Bowl stadium architect Myron Hunt. A long-time Pasadena resident, Myron built this frankly gorgeous house in 1905.

FOOTHILL FREEWAY
ROSEMONT AVENUE
LINCOLN AVENUE
SECO STREET
Brookside Park
LINDA VISTA AVENUE
PROSPECT BLVD
NORTH ORANGE GROVE BLVD
ARROYO TERRACE

An afternoon admiring **architecture in Pasadena**

In the early 1900s, Pasadena became an epicenter of the American Arts and Crafts (or Craftsman) movement. With the city's population growing, new homes were in demand, giving architects the opportunity to run free. The result? Beautiful, decorative, and functional houses, not dissimilar to those designed by fellow Arts and Crafts architects in Britain in the late 1800s. See them for yourself on this dreamy walking tour – just be mindful that many are private homes.

1. Myron Hunt Residence
200 N. Grand Avenue
///fear.zone.axed

2. James A. Culbertson House
235 N. Grand Avenue
///forms.error.elaborate

3. Unitarian Church
1 Westmoreland Place;
www.neighborhooduu.org
///counts.shade.quest

4. The Gamble House
4 Westmoreland Place;
https://gamblehouse.org
///boat.outfit.oasis

5. Millard House
645 Prospect Crescent
///bottle.stay.tanks

6. The Rose Bowl
1001 Rose Bowl Drive
///bill.both.treat

Brookside Golf Club
///snows.oiled.values

NIGHTLIFE

As the sun sets over the Hollywood Hills, the fun is just getting started. Musicians hit the stage, comedians perfect their punch lines, and the city's revelers dance until dawn.

Dinner and a Show

Everything in Los Angeles is a performance, even dinner – here, you don't just get a meal but a full night of entertainment. Dress to impress, bring an appetite, and prepare to expect the unexpected.

CICADA CLUB

Map 1; 617 S. Olive Street, Downtown; ///frame.crowds.incomes; www.cicadaclub.com

If you've ever fantasized about attending a glamorous Old Hollywood party, dream no more: this swanky supper club will transport you straight back to L.A.'s 1920s heyday. Put on your best vintage glad rags, step inside the lavish Art Deco building, and join swingin' revelers dining on tasty Italian food and dancing the night away to live brass bands.

HARVELLE'S

Map 4; 1432 4th Street, Santa Monica; ///weedy.belly.normal; santamonica.harvelles.com

Okay, we're cheating a little bit with this one – Harvelle's doesn't actually serve its own food, but it does let you bring in takeout from the surrounding restaurants. This is dinner and a show

Tickets for Harvelle's are cheaper than at other venues, though most shows here have a two-drink minimum.

dive-style: moody red lighting, cozy tables, and a rough-and-ready mix of comedy, live music, and titillating burlesque performances.

THE MAGIC CASTLE

Map 3; 7001 Franklin Avenue, Hollywood; ///urgent.throw.stones; www.magiccastle.com

Just getting inside this enigmatic clubhouse involves a magic trick – invites are issued by members only. Our advice? Check the lineup and email one of the magicians to ask (nicely) if they can put you on the guest list. Obviously we can't reveal the Magic Castle's secrets, but we can say that dinner and an exclusive show here is one of Hollywood's most memorable nights out.

» Don't leave without popping into Houdini's chamber, which is filled with memorabilia and supposedly still haunted by his ghost.

EL CID

Map 2; 4212 Sunset Boulevard, Silver Lake; ///grow.bonus.strut; www.elcidsunset.com

Pal in need of a pick-me-up? Treat them to a night in Spain at this restaurant and flamenco club. As the dancers clack and twirl across the stage, you'll get to kick back with a glass of sangria and feast on Spanish classics like tapas and paella. Once the show is over, slide across to the pretty outdoor patio where you can catch up over cocktails under the stars.

Solo, Pair, Crowd

Dinner and a show is great for date night, but they can be just as fun if you're on your own or with some pals.

FLYING SOLO

Jazz night

With its low-key setting, Dresden is a perfect spot to catch a show on your own. Movie fans may recognize it as the location where Ron Burgundy (Will Ferrell) performed his jazz flute in *Anchorman*.

IN A PAIR

Old-school romance

Get a taste of classic Hollywood with an old-fashioned date at Miceli's. Here, twinkly lights and singing waitstaff will have you and your partner re-creating that spaghetti scene from *Lady and the Tramp*.

FOR A CROWD

Spooky supper

If you're in need of a scare fix before next Halloween, Beetle House is the place to go. This spooky Tim Burton-themed dinner theater experience is especially fun if you're in a group.

SADDLE RANCH CHOP HOUSE

Map 3; 8371 Sunset Boulevard, West Hollywood; ///clean.brand.quiz; www.thesaddleranch.com

Yes, there's a stage with live fiddlers here, but let's be honest – the show at this Wild West-themed joint is less about the music and more about the mechanical bull. That's right: the mechanical bull. (You may remember it being ridden suggestively by Miranda in an episode of *Sex and the City*.) It's kitsch and it's crude, but the unique blend of hilarity and horror at watching Sunset Strip's party crowd try to channel their inner cowboy is worth the price of the steak alone.

» **Don't leave without** publicly embarrassing yourself on the mechanical bull. This ritual costs about $20 for two rounds – if you can hang on that long.

BLACK RABBIT ROSE

Map 3; 1719 N. Hudson Avenue, Hollywood; ///beyond.move.notice; www.blackrabbitrose.com

Couldn't score an invite to the Magic Castle *(p137)*? Get your sleight-of-hand fix at Black Rabbit Rose. Run by immersive nightlife wizards the Houston brothers (see also Good Times at Davey Wayne's, *p65*), this Victorian-themed lounge feels brimming with secrets from the moment you step among its red velvet drapes. Bartenders conjure up mysterious drinks like the Dark Arts, while a trio of magical artists perform miraculous illusions for well-dressed dates and captivated groups of friends. Prepare to pick a card and have your mind blown.

Comedy Nights

L.A. is the historic home of ha ha, and there's no shortage of places to watch the pros whip up some laughs. For locals, a comedy show is the top go-to for an easy night out.

UCB THEATRE

Map 2; 5919 Franklin Avenue, Hollywood; ///await.fault.agree; www.ucbtheatre.com

Want to know who the next comedy superstar will be? Grab a ticket to a show at the UCB Theatre. It's the performance space for the UCB (Upright Citizens Brigade) comedy school, which is famed as a training ground for the next generation of alternative-skewing funny folk. The school's founders include Amy Poehler and *Veep*

Try it!
TV TAPING

Join the audience for a live TV taping of *Jimmy Kimmel Live* (El Capitan Theater) or *The Late Late Show* (CBS Studios). Tickets for both can be booked via 1iota *(1iota.com)*.

alum Matt Walsh, while Donald Glover and Aubrey Plaza are among those on the impressive alumni list; catch the latest class of improv and sketch students before they graduate to Hollywood.

FLAPPERS

Map 6; 102 E. Magnolia Boulevard, Burbank; ///march.bolt.crab; www.flapperscomedy.com

If you like eating as much as you like laughing, head to Flappers: comedy shows here come with dinner, too (note there's a minimum spend). The level of talent varies wildly – several weekly open mics showcase aspiring acts, while weekend shows typically boast bigger names – but you'll be howling with choke-on-your-food laughter no matter who you see.

THE COMEDY STORE

Map 3; 8433 Sunset Boulevard; West Hollywood; ///fire.exile.judge; www.thecomedystore.com

As much a staple of the raucous Sunset Strip as the nearby rock clubs, The Comedy Store has been on the map ever since Mitzi Shore – legendary comedy impresario and mother to performer Pauly Shore – steered it to success in the 1970s. Any and every comedian worth their salt has performed on the main stage or in the more intimate Belly Room – just check out the legions of A-listers' signatures on the outside of the venue for proof.

» **Don't leave without** staying to the bitter end of the show – big-name surprise guests are known to drop in at any point.

LAUGH FACTORY

Map 3; 8001 Sunset Boulevard, West Hollywood; ///helps.roses.mint; www.laughfactory.com

Never has a venue's name been quite so on point. The Laugh Factory's lineup is a rotating conveyor belt of household-name stand-ups, whose top-of-the-range performances provoke huge quantities of gasping-for-air laughter.

CHATTERBOX COMEDY

Map 6; 943 N. Citrus Avenue, Covina; ///agrees.families.terminal; (626) 331-7500

Every Sunday, a quirky audience who prefer their comedy to be less mainstream and more wild venture out to this welcoming dive bar in the suburbs of San Gabriel Valley. And they're never disappointed. The lineups of unknowns are where you're sure to find your next favorite performer.

THE GROUNDLINGS THEATRE

Map 3; 7307 Melrose Avenue, West Hollywood; ///retire.occupy.fires; www.groundlings.com

Will Ferrell. Melissa McCarthy. Maya Rudolph. Kristen Wiig. The list of performers who got their start at this seminal venue reads like a who's who of comedy A-listers. Weekend shows with the main company draw the crowds, but any night here will have you in stitches.

» **Don't leave without** pausing to pay tribute at the plaque to The Groundlings' founder and original director, Gary Austin.

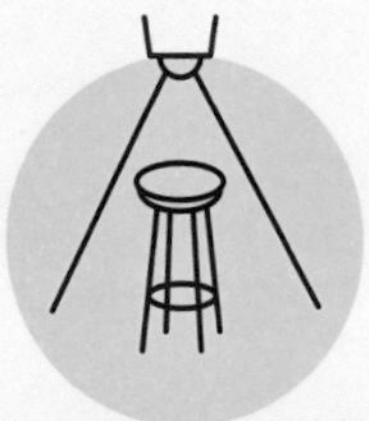

Liked by the locals

"If you're looking for a witty evening, you have to stop by The Groundlings Theatre on Melrose. With improv and sketch shows happening weekly, this theater is a Hollywood staple."

CARRIE LAFERLE GERGELY,
MANAGING DIRECTOR OF THE GROUNDLINGS

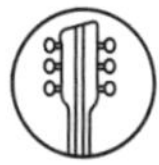

Music Venues

From hair metal to folk rock to gangster rap, L.A.'s neighborhood venues have been the birthplace of generations of popular music. Catch local bands and touring acts at the city's best live music spots.

RESIDENT

Map 1; 428 S. Hewitt Street, Arts District; ///span.sock.knee; www.residentdtla.com

Resident feels more like a festival space than a concert venue, so do the sensible thing and make a gig here an all-day event. Rock up in the afternoon for a drink in the beer garden, grab dinner from one of the rotating food trucks, then head inside for a blast of whatever genre-pushing act is playing that night (it can be anything from psych to soul to hip-hop). Finish with a cozy cocktail next to the firepits.

THE SARDINE

Map 5; 1101 S. Pacific Avenue, San Pedro; ///carb.petition.towards; www.thesardinepedro.com

Get your best pogo moves ready for a night of punk rock at this combined venue, record store, and neighborhood bar. Small, hot, and fantastically loud, it's packed with South Bay residents of all

The Sardine isn't just open for shows. You can buy some vinyl or grab a beer on the patio any time.

ages rocking out to noisy bands. If you're not dripping with sweat by the time the show's over, we'll be extremely disappointed.

WALT DISNEY CONCERT HALL

Map 1; 111 S. Grand Avenue, Downtown; ///loaf.funny.goals; www.laphil.com

Think classical music is stuffy? The Frank Gehry-designed Walt Disney Concert Hall is here to change your mind. Okay, it still offers plenty of Mozart and Beethoven, but you'll also find experimental modern works and fun holiday-themed shows. Our favorite event is the Casual Friday concert series – it includes a free (yes, free) post-show beer tasting with members of the orchestra.

» Don't leave without checking out the Blue Ribbon Garden, a hidden rooftop oasis dedicated to Lillian Disney.

THE ECHO + ECHOPLEX

Map 1; 1822 W. Sunset Boulevard, Echo Park; ///saying.firm.hype; www.theecho.com

This is, in fact, not one venue but two: The Echo, a dance floor-size bar on the street level, and Echoplex, an underground nightclub below. Every night brings a different crowd to both, depending on which reggae/dub DJ or indie band is playing. It's good to grab a ticket in advance, even if the scenester, go-with-the-flow Echo Park crowd gives off the vibe of not being the type to plan things in advance.

TROUBADOUR

Map 3; 9081 N. Santa Monica Boulevard, West Hollywood; ///nodded.humans.avoid; www.troubadour.com

If you're on the hunt for a slice of the city's music history, head to this iconic venue. Both Elton John and Guns N' Roses were catapulted to superstardom from here, and it's still the best place in town to check out up-and-coming talent. As you wait for the music to start, follow in the footsteps of Don Henley and Glenn Frey and grab a drink at the front bar – that's how the pair met in 1970, before going on to make music legend as the Eagles.

HOLLYWOOD BOWL

Map 3; 2301 N. Highland Avenue, Hollywood Hills; ///sing.fats.reward; www.hollywoodbowl.com

Come summer, the Hollywood Bowl is *the* date venue for the city's desperate-to-impress romantics. A classical performance from the L.A. Philharmonic, a show by a big-name pop artist, or a celebration of Hollywood's iconic soundtracks – the music may change nightly, but the magic of a concert under the stars is always the same.

THE SMELL

Map 1; 247 S. Main Street, Downtown; ///fruit.forest.tower; www.thesmell.org

The Smell has got all the grunge you'd expect of a DIY punk and experimental venue (back-alley entrance, graffitied walls), but with the unforeseen twist of a booze-free, all-ages door policy. This is the sort of place where you enter the underground music scene as a curious teen, and return as a jaded adult to blow off steam with a night of thrashing to loud, messy tunes.

THE ROXY

Map 3; 9009 Sunset Boulevard, West Hollywood; ///sushi.became.assume; www.theroxy.com

The legendary Sunset Strip might not be quite the incubator of arena-ready talent it once was, but the intimate Roxy is still doing the neighborhood's musical legacy proud. On any given night, an eclectic mix of locals can be found swaying to the melodies of singer-songwriters, bouncing around to hip-hop beats, or nodding energetically to the sounds of indie rock.

» **Don't leave without** visiting some of the Strip's other famous venues, including Whisky a Go Go and the Viper Room.

Thousands of Angelenos go to the movie screenings at Hollywood Forever Cemetery *(p125)*, but only a select group of music fans nab tickets to gigs at the cemetery's Masonic Lodge *(hollywoodforever.com)*. This atmospheric hall is about as cozy and intimate as venues get, with a wooden-beamed ceiling, candelabra lights, and only 150 tickets available per show. Think stripped-back, bare-your-soul sets from a mix of indie artists standing only yards away.

LGBTQ+ Scene

West Hollywood might be the center of LGBTQ+ life for many Angelenos, but the entire city has vibrant pockets that revel in queer culture, with nonstop dancing, loud music, and late nights.

HAMBURGER MARY'S

Map 5; 330 Pine Avenue, Long Beach; ///discount.lamp.backup; www.hamburgermarys.com

Hamburger might be in the name, but really people pack this place for everything but the food. The flamboyant bar and nightclub is front and center of Long Beach's gay scene, drawing a fun-loving crowd with some of the country's best-loved drag acts. Arrive early to get a great seat, bring plenty of dollar bills for tipping the performers, and be sure to order the orange creamsicle cocktail.

THE ABBEY

Map 3; 692 N. Robertson Boulevard, West Hollywood; ///glad.cliff.lonely; www.theabbeyweho.com

You wouldn't know it listening to the thumping pop music beats or watching the thrusting dancers on stage, but The Abbey started out as a modest coffee shop. It was opened in 1991, in the midst of the

AIDS crisis, as a safe space for gay men to be themselves and find a sense of community. And boy did it prove popular: The Abbey has since expanded five times (it's now the largest gay bar in WeHo) and is treasured as the heart of the area's LGBTQ+ scene.

HI TOPS

Map 3; 8933 Santa Monica Boulevard, West Hollywood; ///output.laser.fears; www.hitopsbar.com

With its cheeky name and locker-room aesthetic, this friendly WeHo sports bar is a laid-back spot to watch the game on a Sunday. Cheer on L.A.'s beloved Rams while sipping zingy cocktails and snacking on surprisingly good bar food (try the grilled cauliflower on a stick). Whose house? Rams' house!

» Don't leave without **staying for happy hour – it's one of the best in West Hollywood, with $5 beers and bubbly.**

CATCH ONE

Map 4; 4067 W. Pico Boulevard, Arlington Heights; ///foster.sofa.costs; www.catch.one

Catch One is an L.A. institution. Founded back in 1973 by Jewel Thais-Williams, it was one of the first Black-owned discos in the country. Known then as Jewel's Catch One, the club essentially pioneered L.A.'s Black LGBTQ+ scene and became a legend of city nightlife (there's even a whole Netflix documentary about the place). Jewel herself is no longer running the joint (hence the current name), but her inclusive spirit lives on.

PRECINCT

Map 1; 357 S. Broadway, Downtown; ///enhancement.feed.colleague; www.precinctdtla.com

Downtown finally has a massive, multiroom, party-focused gay club to rival the ones in WeHo: Precinct. Expect a trendy industrial aesthetic, cheap drinks, and a relaxed crowd where everyone just wants to blow off some steam.

AKBAR

Map 2; 4356 W. Sunset Boulevard, Silver Lake; ///sadly.cabin.fills; www.akbarsilverlake.com

Gyrating gogo dancers not your thing? Bypass West Hollywood and hit up this unpretentious spot in Silver Lake. Eastsiders adore Akbar for its intimate, neighborhood vibe, with a crowd that's always welcoming and a dance floor that's always jumping to an epic mix of tunes.

» **Don't leave without** wandering into the back room to select some tunes on the beloved jukebox.

QUE SERA

Map 5; 1923 E. 7th Street, Long Beach; ///full.skip.bribing; www.queseralb.com

Run by a team of no-nonsense-but-kind lesbians, this divey bar is all about live shows: mainly music (singer Melissa Ethridge got her start here), but also comedy and a bit of burlesque. It's dark, loud, and just how the regulars like it – especially when it comes to the heavy-handed pours at the bar.

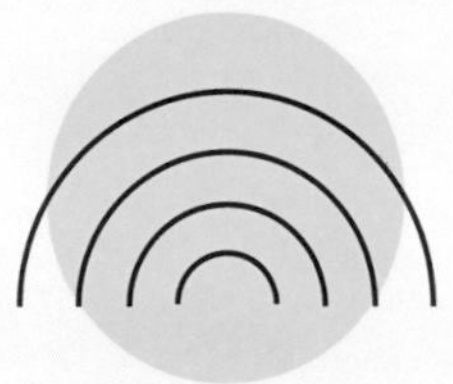

Liked by the locals

"Precinct is special because it's a space in L.A. gay culture where all types of queer people can fit in and feel at ease. It also happens to be the best place for drag queen sightings. I once saw Trixie Mattel and Jackie Beat in one weekend."

REBECCA KRAMER,
EXECUTIVE ASSISTANT

Cool Clubs

Ready to shake it to cumbia, EDM, or hip-hop? L.A.'s expansive club scene has you covered. Whatever your jam, you'll find a spot to strut your stuff.

PANAMERICAN NIGHT CLUB

Map 1; 2601 W. Temple Street, Westlake; ///assets.enhancement.focus; www.panamericannightclub.com

If you're looking to party to some Latin beats, Panamerican is the place to be. Every day here brings a different sound – there's parranda on Wednesdays, tropical night on Fridays, and rumba on Sundays, plus countless other genres on the days in between. Come dressed to the nines and ready to show off your moves.

SHORT STOP

Map 1; 1455 W. Sunset Boulevard, Echo Park; ///alone.oiled.tigers; www.instagram.com/theshortstopechopark

By day, this neighborhood dive bar is a pregame staple for baseball fans heading to nearby Dodger Stadium (hence the name). By night, however, it morphs into a pumping dance destination filled with Echo Park hipsters out for a good time.

The music changes daily, but some things are guaranteed: cheap drinks, a nonjudgmental crowd, and almost certainly at least one person on the dance floor in a Dodgers cap.

LA CITA

Map 1; 336 S. Hill Street, Downtown; ///cool.punk.influencing; www.lacitabar.com

We don't like to brag, but La Cita has twice appeared in *Esquire* magazine's "Best Bars in America" feature. Not to say that means you'll get high-end gloss here: this place is classic dive bar, complete with all the sweat and red neon lights that entails. It's the fun atmosphere and live music that make it special, with a lineup of cumbia legends, local bands, and DJs loved by everyone from abuelos in cowboy hats to excitable 20-somethings.

» **Don't leave without** **taking a breather in El Patio at the back, an airy outdoor space that has a more low-key DJ vibe to the one inside.**

It's generally accepted that hitting a club in L.A. requires putting on your most expensive clothes and doing your best to impress everyone you encounter. Not so at Bootie L.A. *(bootie mashup.com)*, a scene-y but still surprisingly low-key club night that rotates through a few key spots. You can count on eclectic mash-ups featuring unlikely pairings of pop, rock, and rap, enjoyed by a crowd of irony-loving locals.

EXCHANGE LA

Map 1; 618 S. Spring Street, Downtown; ///dame.brave.glad; exchangela.com

If you've always wanted to re-create Coachella's famed Sahara tent – full of fashionable, care-free people in the biggest dance frenzy imaginable – this massive club in Downtown is for you. Spread over four stories in the former L.A. Stock Exchange building, it's packed with party-focused clubbers and EDM fans of all stripes losing themselves wildly to the music.

ZEBULON

Map 2; 2478 Fletcher Drive, Frogtown; ///origin.online.hours; zebulon.la

For East Coast transplants seeking out Big Apple vibes, Zebulon quickly cures any homesickness – once based in hipster-central Williamsburg, it's found a new home in similarly trendy Frogtown. Industrial-style decor? Check. On-trend DJs and theme nights? Check. A too-cool-to-care crowd casually letting their hair down? Double check. Who needs rainy old New York, anyway?

SKYBAR

Map 3; 8440 Sunset Boulevard, West Hollywood; ///tiles.saving.locals; www.sbe.com

Come prepared to give off your most nonchalant, over-it L.A. vibe imaginable. This glitzy rooftop destination on Sunset Boulevard comes with a high-glam atmosphere soundtracked by a mix of rap

and house music. It's the haunt of the rich, young, and extremely well-connected, and if you're in the mood for bottle service, you can't do much better.

AVALON HOLLYWOOD

Map 3; 1735 Vine Street, Hollywood; ///crown.intent.nuns; avalonhollywood.com

Tinseltown is constantly reinventing itself, and the Avalon is no exception. Having hosted Lucille Ball's radio show, The Beatles' first West Coast appearance, and The Ramones' final concert, this historic venue found new life in the 2000s as one of L.A.'s best superclubs. Expect high-profile DJs, a sound system that'll leave your ears buzzing, and a gleeful, dance-like-nobody's-watching energy.

» Don't leave without seeing if you can guess the spot in the main theater where a pre-presidential Richard Nixon gave his famous "Checkers speech" back in 1952.

THE VIRGIL

Map 2; 4519 Santa Monica Boulevard, East Hollywood; ///magma.nest.gets; www.thevirgil.com

This Hollywood hole-in-the-wall may be little, but it packs a punch. Drag artists, comedians, and musicians rotate on the main stage, drawing a consistently cool crowd, but it's the themed club nights you don't want to miss (picture DJs spinning queer pop bangers, indie sleaze classics, and the best of Taylor Swift).

0 meters 400
0 yards 400

Whisky a Go Go
has been a rock 'n' roll Sunset Strip staple since 1964. Famously, it once had The Doors as its house band.

WEST SUNSE

Close out the night
BARNEY'S BEANER

This L.A. staple isn't the mo
refined, but after a night of high jin
a relaxed watering hole with tab
games is maybe just what you nee

WEST SUNSET BOULEVARD

HOLLOWAY DRIVE

PALM AVENUE

SANTA MONICA BOULEVARD

WEST HOLLYWOOD

NORTH LA CIENEGA BOULEVARD

HUNTLEY DRIVE

Dance with abandon at
ROCCO'S

Located along the buzzy stretch of Santa Monica Boulevard (known colloquially as Boys Town), this raucous gay club is co-owned by *NSYNC's Lance Bass.

3

2

NORTH SAN VICENTE BLVD

Raise a glass at
HI TOPS

This gay sports bar always promises a good time. Order a sports-themed cocktail and be sure to line your stomach with stadium favorites like pretzels and pork chops on a stick.

1

Enjoy the scenery at
CATCH LA

There's no better place to see and be seen than at this rooftop bar and restaurant. Indulge in a cocktail and seafood with a view, and keep your eyes peeled for celebrities doing the same (reservations are a must).

MELROSE AVENUE

Mobster Bugsy Siegel lived at what's today **Tower Bar**, *in the Sunset Tower Hotel. John Wayne and Frank Sinatra also called this spot home.*

A night out in West Hollywood

The folk of West Hollywood (or WeHo) have long been a rebellious bunch. In the 1920s, rather than have their patch incorporated into the City of Los Angeles, locals opted to remain under the jurisdiction of L.A. County. Gambling was illegal in the city, you see, so casinos and nightclubs thrived here, especially along Sunset Boulevard. WeHo residents still love a good time, spending their evenings partying at scene-y bars, swinging LGBTQ+ nightclubs, and welcoming dives.

1. Catch LA
8715 Melrose Avenue; www.catchrestaurants.com
///forks.hurt.agree

2. Hi Tops
8933 Santa Monica Boulevard; hitopsbar.com
///also.plenty.spite

3. Rocco's
8900 Santa Monica Boulevard; www.roccosweho.com
///codes.roses.return

4. Barney's Beanery
8447 Santa Monica Boulevard; https://barneysbeanery.com
///shout.clown.ocean

Tower Bar
///stocks.total.valve

Whisky a Go Go
///lobby.blitz.basis

OUTDOORS

Surf, sand, and almost year-round sun – outdoor living is what L.A.'s all about. Whether they're lazing on the beach or hiking in the hills, Angelenos are always found outside.

Beautiful Beaches

You can't come to L.A. and not dip your toes in the ocean. Everyone knows about the famous beaches of Venice and Santa Monica, but here's where the locals go when they want to avoid the crowds.

PENINSULA BAYSIDE BEACH

Map 5; E. Bayshore Walk between 55th Place and 68th Place, Long Beach; ///desktop.strict.material

Looking for a quiet spot to chill with a good book? Head east on Ocean Boulevard until you hit The Peninsula. This thin strip of land is barely two blocks wide, with upscale houses down the center and tranquil sandy beaches on either side. You can lay your towel out anywhere, but those in the know go for the northern coast, facing

Try it!
GO FOR A PADDLE

If you're feeling energetic, Bayside Beach is a great place from which to go kayaking or paddleboarding for a few hours. Rentals are available year-round near Bayshore Park, at the start of The Peninsula.

Alamitos Bay (hence, Bayside Beach). That way, you can while away the hours without getting sand blown in your paperback by the afternoon winds that whip the Pacific side.

BURNOUT BEACH

Map 5; 1801 Esplanade, Redondo Beach; ///cage.drives.newly

Locals can't agree how this surfer's haven got its name (some say it's a reference to a historic fire, others a nod to the bonfire parties held here), but we can guarantee it's not an indictment of the caliber of people who frequent it. Here, you'll encounter L.A. beach life at its laid-back best: swimmers and surfers bobbing in the waves, couples strolling hand in hand, and groups of friends just chilling in the sun.

BRUCE'S BEACH

Map 4; 2600 Highland Avenue, Manhattan Beach; ///wakes.normal.amuse

You won't just find sand at Bruce's Beach, you'll uncover some important history, too. In the early 1900s, ambitious couple Willa and Charles Bruce established a thriving seaside resort here for Manhattan Beach's Black community. Within a few decades, however, white residents had run the business out of town and local government seized the land for a park. Ownership of the property was finally returned to the Bruce family in 2021; for now, it remains a peaceful spot to ponder the past while overlooking the ocean.

» **Don't leave without** pausing to read the plaque in the middle of the park that tells the Bruces' story.

LEO CARRILLO STATE PARK

Map 6; 35000 Pacific Coast Highway, Malibu; ///fuss.chemicals.irritant

Want to enjoy a beach day with your four-legged partner-in-crime? Then you'll love this serene stretch of sand. As one of the few beaches in Los Angeles that welcomes dogs (they just have to be on a leash, and you'll need to stay between lifeguard towers three and four), it draws pets and their owners from all over.

ZUMA BEACH

Map 6; 30000 Pacific Coast Highway, Malibu; ///transcript.avert.mavericks; beaches.lacounty.gov/zuma-beach

Cruise up the Pacific Coast Highway, past the moneyed mansions of Malibu, and keep going until you're almost at the Ventura County line. There you'll find the cleanest (and coldest) 2 miles (3 km) of ocean water in L.A. Zuma Beach is long, wide, and comes with big waves that are perfect for board sports. If you want to get a taste of California surf culture, this is the place to post up.

SOUTH BEACH SANTA MONICA

Map 4; 3400 Barnard Way, Santa Monica; ///limit.client.robot

We get it – you want to see if Santa Monica and Venice live up to the hype. Well (spoiler alert), they do, but they're pretty much always packed with people. So once you're done checking out the boardwalk and pier, stake out a space for the rest of the day on this stretch of sand and parkland between the two. Comparatively free of tourists, it draws a low-key crowd of runners out on their daily jog,

Hit up Main Street in Santa Monica for the best bars and shops on the south side of the 10 Freeway.

families hitting the seaside playground, and kids from across L.A. riding bikes down the historic beach path. It's a relative haven of calm amid the chaos.

OCEAN TRAILS RESERVE

Map 5; 1 Trump National Drive, Rancho Palos Verdes; ///lifelike.drillers.wayward; rpvca.gov/1154/Ocean-Trails-Reserve

Sometimes, when you've had a bad week, all you want to do is escape the city and lose yourself in nature. At these moments, the Ocean Trails Reserve is the perfect tonic. Part rolling hills pocked with fancy mansions and part network of protected lands, it's laced with paths along breathtaking bluffs. Hike down the cliffs to surround yourself with native sea life and soothing ocean views. By the time high tide washes you back out and up to your car, you'll feel as good as new.

» **Don't leave without** grabbing a sandwich for lunch at Busy Bee, on your way through nearby San Pedro.

DOCKWEILER STATE BEACH

Map 4; 12000 Vista del Mar, Playa del Rey; ///flame.spits.gloves; beaches.lacounty.gov/dockweiler-beach

Behind you is a power plant and overhead are the planes taking off from LAX – but in front of you lies glorious open sea, with miles of sandy beach stretching out to either side. It's about as real as the beach in L.A. gets, and everyone who comes here to roast marshmallows on the bonfire pits knows it.

Green Spaces

Sure, San Francisco has Golden Gate Park, but L.A.'s gone one better with large, grassy expanses in every part of town. Park culture here is all about relaxing – enjoying some greenery while soaking up the sun.

ERNEST E. DEBS PARK

Map 6; 4235 Monterey Road, Montecito Hills; ///little.react.pets; www.laparks.org

Debs Park is the ultimate symbol of L.A.'s community spirit and love of the outdoors. It's the hiking groups that meet weekly to trek through the natural arroyo woodlands – among the last in Southern California. It's the families who gather at the picnic sites to catch up while the kids play and birds flit overhead. And it's the volunteers who inspire locals to care for the natural world at the Audubon Center (in the U.S.'s first carbon-neutral building, no less).

ECHO PARK LAKE

Map 1; 751 Echo Park Avenue, Echo Park; ///fees.dare.almost

This centerpiece of the Echo Park neighborhood is one of L.A.'s original builds, dating back to 1860. It's been a hub for residents ever since, where impressive views of the Downtown skyline backdrop lush

Get out on the lake in one of the swan-shaped pedal boats – it's a fun way to enjoy the water.

strolls along the water. Pass the day here reading on the grass and tucking into *elotes* (corn) and *paletas* (popsicles) from roaming street food vendors.

GRAND PARK

Map 1; 200 N. Grand Avenue, Downtown; ///dined.lasted.cans; www.grandparkla.org

In the shadow of City Hall, this strip of grass prides itself on being "the park for everyone." It's a microcosm of L.A.'s people and their interests – a public square to come together for protests, concerts, and an annual New Year's Eve light display. Events aside, it's simply a much-needed bit of greenery where office workers hang on their lunch break, children splash in the fountain, and visiting couples look to re-create the romantic moments filmed here for *Pretty Woman*.

GRIFFITH PARK

Map 2; 4730 Crystal Springs Drive, Los Feliz; ///pies.leave.skill; www.laparks.org

Angelenos are quick to boast that Griffith Park is five times the size of N.Y.C.'s famed Central Park. And, as the largest park in L.A., it tends to be every local's favorite green space. Pretty much all walks of life are found here, from the Los Feliz hipsters on their look-at-me morning cardio sessions to the families who hit up L.A. Zoo on the weekend.

» **Don't leave without** hiking to Amir's Garden, a serene oasis where flowers and jaw-dropping views of the city and mountains await.

Solo, Pair, Crowd

L.A. has plenty of places where you and your friends can get away from the concrete jungle.

FLYING SOLO

Beautiful blooms

Take some time out in Exposition Park and stop to (literally) smell the roses. From December to April, the Rose Garden here blooms with around 16,000 flowers, creating a heavenly setting for a bit of me-time.

IN A PAIR

Gossip and greenery

With its lush foliage, peaceful paths, and pretty water features, Los Angeles County Arboretum is a cute spot to meet up with a pal. Find a bench in a shady nook and catch up on all the latest gossip.

FOR A CROWD

Fun among the flowers

Gather the gang to play hide-and-seek at the South Coast Botanic Garden. Eight sculptures have been hidden among the foliage, and guests of all ages are encouraged to go and hunt for them.

DESCANSO GARDENS

Map 6; 1418 Descanso Drive, La Cañada Flintridge; ///ranch.text.life; www.descansogardens.org

A love for plants has always been at the heart of Descanso, from its early days as a private garden to its 1950 adoption as a public space. It remains a place for nature-loving folk, to wander through oak forests or breathe in the aroma of fruit trees. Heavenly.

HUNTINGTON LIBRARY

Map 6; 1151 Oxford Road, San Marino; ///note.going.awake; www.huntington.org

The former estate of railroad magnate Henry Huntington is now a museum, but many locals bypass the interior for an amble around the gardens. And why not? There are lots of lush themed areas, including a desert garden and a Japanese garden, to name just a couple.

» Don't leave without checking out the museum. It's got a collection of notable artwork, plus an original copy of the Gutenberg Bible.

ELYSIAN PARK

Map 1; 929 Academy Road, Elysian Park; ///plan.brains.priced; www.laparks.org

Angelenos are passionate about the Dodgers, so it's no surprise that they love this park, too – it's home to Dodger Stadium *(p174)*. On game days, you'll find the grass covered in high-spirited baseball fans; the rest of the time, it's sprinkled with joggers, hikers, and cyclists, enjoying views of the city as they hit the trails.

Heavenly Hikes

They say Angelenos never walk anywhere, but we're here to tell you different. Come the weekend, locals swap the concrete jungle for the dirt trails and fresh air of the city's beautiful public nature reserves.

RUNYON CANYON

Map 3; start at 2000 N. Fuller Avenue, Hollywood Hills; ///diner.flats.steer

This isn't one for lacing up your muddy boots: Runyon Canyon is all about seeing and being seen. That means donning your best yoga pants and designer sneakers for the 2.7-mile (4.3-km) loop, along which you're likely to spot a celebrity or two walking their pooch. Once you reach the top, though, you won't care a jot about the up-and-coming actor you might have seen along the way – it's the pools and houses dotting the Hollywood hills that will have your full attention.

CHANTRY FLAT

Map 6; Chantry Flat Road, Arcadia; ///fully.goatskin.buffets

Chantry Flat has a lot going for it. First off, it's home to the last donkey-packing station in the San Gabriel Mountains, reminiscent of a time when freight was transported via pack animal. Secondly, it's the trailhead for the rugged but beautiful Gabrielino Trail, which

Get there early. The parking lot fills up fast, so if you're late, you'll have to park lower down and hike up.

winds past century-old settler cabins on the way to Mt. Wilson. The 15-mile (24-km) hike to the summit is a killer, but the views throughout are totally worth it.

CULVER CITY STAIRS

Map 4; start at Jefferson Boulevard, Culver City; ///spout.poker.fortunate

Stairs might not ordinarily scream "hike," but this outdoor staircase is notorious for being quite the workout. Also known as the Baldwin Hills Scenic Overlook, it's always bustling with L.A. fitness fanatics getting their cardio in, either running or power-walking up the 282 uneven steps to the top. Shaky knees are guaranteed by the end, so take a moment of rest and soak up the amazing views of L.A. below.

» **Don't leave without** walking to downtown Culver City after to reward yourself with brunch – you'll need the carbs, right?

STOUGH CANYON

Map 6; start at 2300 E. Walnut Avenue, Burbank; ///marked.boxer.second

Looking for a family-friendly hike around the hills? Head to Stough Canyon in Burbank. This rugged area promises walking trails for all abilities, with some easy routes (there's a lovely half-hour trail to a viewpoint) offering stunning views over the San Fernando Valley. Before you set off, however, be sure to pop into the Stough Canyon Nature Center. Located at the start of the trailhead, this educational center features exhibits on the area's wildflowers and wildlife – some of which you'll hopefully spot on your walk.

TURNBULL CANYON

Map 6; start on Turnbull Canyon Road, Whittier; ///residual.crops.subsets

Ask the locals about Turnbull Canyon and they'll likely have a tall tale to tell. The hills of this Whittier nature reserve are shrouded in urban legend: ghosts are said to lurk in the shadows, while secret tunnels are rumored to exist beneath the ground. Whether that's true or not, there's one thing no-one can deny: the canyon offers some of L.A.'s most spectacular scenery. Follow the 4-mile (6-km) loop up the hills and you'll be rewarded with epic views over the San Gabriel Valley.

LOS LIONES

Map 6; start on 510 Los Liones Drive, Pacific Palisades; ///held.awake.active

It might be a short 3-mile (5-km) route, but you have to work hard on this grueling hike. There are plenty of brutal switchbacks (trails that cut suddenly from one direction to the next while ascending a sharp incline) and not a ton of shade, so pack plenty of water and

If you want a cool desert vibe without going all the way to Joshua Tree National Park, head just north of L.A. to Vasquez Rocks. It has a great selection of hiking trails and lots of stunning, otherworldly sandstone formations. You'll likely recognize the scenery: it's starred in numerous movies and TV shows including *Star Trek*, *Westworld*, and *Buffy the Vampire Slayer*, to name just a few.

sunscreen. A bench at the end of the trail offers respite for those burning calves, while you soak up rad views of the Pacific. Little wonder the trail is loved by those seeking another reason to show off that they live in L.A. (as if they need one).

SOLSTICE CANYON

Map 6; start on Solstice Canyon Road, Malibu; ///abide.paddock.loners

You'll rarely hear locals complaining about the weather, but a bit of shade from the blazing sun is always welcome. This easy 3-mile (5-km) stroll through the former grounds of a Malibu estate offers just that, with shaded paths and streams and small pools to cool off in. It feels worlds away from the nearby packed beaches – though you'll still get a taste of the ocean with the awesome views.

» Don't leave without seeing the rare year-round waterfall at the back of the property.

WISDOM TREE HIKE

Map 6; start on Lake Hollywood Drive, Hollywood Hills; ///jams.cloak.lucky

At the top of Burbank Peak stands L.A.'s most resilient tree, the lone survivor of a devastating wildfire. The trek up to it is steep, but short, and promises some of the best 360-degree views in the city. But that's not even the best part. Beneath the tree you'll find an ammo box stuffed with dozens of guest books that read like a collective diary of Angelenos' hopes, dreams, and terrible jokes. Bring a pen along with you and contribute some words of wisdom – you never know who'll read them, or who'll need them.

Live Sports Venues

The Lakers, the Dodgers, the Rams: you've probably heard of L.A.'s iconic sports teams, but have you seen them play live? Nab a ticket and you're in for a whirlwind of emotion, fuelled by plenty of gametime snacks.

SURFING AT HUNTINGTON BEACH

Map 6; 315 Pacific Coast Highway, Huntington Beach; ///insiders.clings.animated; www.surfcityusa.com

Every summer since 1959, Huntington Beach (a.k.a "Surf City U.S.A.") has become the epicenter of the U.S. Open, the world's largest surfing competition. During the week-long event, the coast transforms with live music, food trucks, and surfing so good it'll make you gasp. The best viewing spots are halfway down the pier, where you can catch the occasional dolphin pod weaving among the competitors.

FOOTBALL AT SOFI STADIUM

Map 4; 1001 Stadium Drive, Inglewood; ///mice.notion.relates; www.sofistadium.com

When your stadium costs $5 billion, you'd better believe it's impressive. The SoFi has capacity for a staggering 70,240 fans, but the real showstopper is the Infinity Screen – a 360-degree,

70,000-sq-ft- (6,500 sq-m-) video board that makes even nose-bleed seats feel premium. Both the Los Angeles Rams and the Chargers play here; the former promises full-on spectacle (think elaborate pre-game shows and celebrity sightings), while the latter offer a more laid-back vibe and better ticket prices.

BASKETBALL AT THE CRYPTO.COM ARENA

Map 1; 1111 S. Figueroa Street, Downtown; ///delay.fantastic.inches; www.cryptoarena.com

One of the most successful teams in history, the Lakers are no ordinary basketball team, and "the house that Kobe built" is no ordinary arena. This sprawling indoor space – home to a statue memorializing the late, great Kobe Bryant – promises an electric atmosphere whatever the game. Its courtside seats are basically an extension of Hollywood, too (if the game gets dull, try counting celebrities).

» **Don't leave without** booking tickets for an L.A. Sparks games – the WNBA team also plays here and tickets are a steal.

ANGEL CITY FC AT BMO STADIUM

Map 4; 3939 S. Figueroa Street, Exposition Park; ///silks.face.orders; www.angelcity.com

Tickets to see this women's soccer team have quickly become the hottest in town, partly because of the Fan Fest held before major matches. Rock up early to enjoy the DJs and food trucks, and mingle with celebs (co-owner Natalie Portman often stops by) and fans alike.

DODGERS AT THE DODGER STADIUM

Map 1; 1000 Vin Scully Avenue, Elysian Park; ///dame.poppy.cotton; www.mlb.com/dodgers

There's baseball, and then there's Dodgers baseball. Playing in the third-oldest ballpark in the MLB, L.A.'s beloved team are so popular that even the sports-adverse can't resist making the pilgrimage to this retro stadium. Join the time-honored tradition of arriving fashionably late and leaving early (blame the traffic), bellowing baseball chants, and bobbing up and down whenever the wave makes its way around.

» **Don't leave without** grabbing a Dodger dog and garlic fries – you'll need fuel for all the excitement and these gametime snacks are nearly as iconic as the team itself.

ROSE BOWL GAME

Map 6; 1001 Rose Bowl Drive, Pasadena; ///bend.spider.donor; www.rosebowlstadium.com

New Year's Day in L.A. means one thing: the Rose Bowl Game. Known as "The Granddaddy of Them All," America's oldest bowl tradition began in 1902 and has been hosted in this vast stadium for most of its history. While the game – an extravagant battle between two college football powerhouses – is the main event, there's plenty to see in the lead up. Earlier in the day, there's the Tournament of Roses Parade, a display of flower-covered floats and marching bands in Pasadena. And before that it's decorating week, where visitors can go behind-the-scenes to watch volunteers crafting the elaborate floats from fresh flowers.

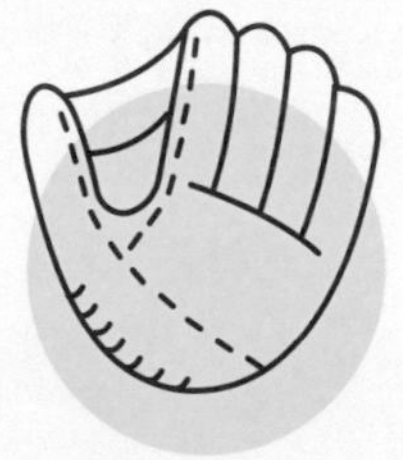

Liked by the locals

"One of the fastest – and most enjoyable – ways to get to get to know L.A. culture is to go to a Dodgers game. You get to cheer alongside friends and strangers, eat all the snacks, and do the wave! What's not to love?"

JUSTINE HIPSKY,
WRITER

Movie Magic

Getting déjà vu while checking out L.A.? It's probably because you're somewhere that you've seen on screen. Industry icons are sprinkled all over town – these are our favorite, most easily accessible spots.

GRIFFITH OBSERVATORY

Map 2; 2800 East Observatory Road, Griffith Park; ///lime.liner.organs; griffithobservatory.org

As if the great views weren't enough of a reason to visit this storied observatory, it's also been a location for some of Hollywood's most memorable scenes. Come here to live out your best *La La Land* fantasy, or rail against the world like James Dean in *Rebel Without a Cause*. Just watch out for the dinosaurs (only kidding) – the building also played the welcome center in *Jurassic Park*.

CIRCUS LIQUOR

Map 6; 5600 Vineland Avenue, North Hollywood; ///heap.kicked.racing; circusliquor.gotoliquorstore.com

Remember that scene in *Clueless* where Cher gets mugged? Well, the parking lot outside this liquor store is where it happened. (You'll know you're in the right place when you spot the giant neon sign featuring a rather menacing clown.) Admittedly, it's not the most glamorous movie location we could have chosen, but it's a signature landmark of the Valley – and *Clueless* is a 90s icon of Valley life. So, like, whatever.

POINT DUME

Map 6; Westward Beach Road, Malibu; ///nicer.fuel.reroute

If you're a Marvel fan, you may recognize this rocky promontory as the location of Tony Stark's coastal mansion in the *Iron Man* movies. But that's not Point Dume's most famous cinematic cameo; it was also the setting for the pivotal final scene in the original *Planet of the Apes.* We won't spoil the ending for you, but let's just say it's nearly as startling as the views here.

» **Don't leave without** making an appointment to tour the nearby Melody Ranch Studio, where countless Westerns have been filmed.

BRADBURY BUILDING

Map 1; 304 S. Broadway, Downtown; ///shop.result.shadow; www.laconservancy.org/locations/bradbury-building

Even if you don't know the Bradbury Building by name, it'll definitely look familiar when you step inside. The atrium of this National Historic Landmark – with its distinctive staircases and ironwork – has supplied the backdrop for everything from *Blade Runner* to *The Artist*, not to mention countless music videos. It's a working office building, but you're free to go inside and have a wander around the first floor – unless it's closed for filming, of course.

USC CAMPUS

Map 4; University Park Campus, University Park; ///react.cone.hills; www.usc.edu

If you've ever seen students hurrying to class on the big screen, chances are they were filmed at USC. Its lovely campus and central L.A. location make it a prime pick for college footage. It's even stood in for other real-life schools – like in Forrest Gump's graduation scene, where it filled in for the University of Alabama, and key moments from *Legally Blonde*, where it substituted for Harvard.

HOLLYWOOD SIGN

Map 2; 5600 Sunset Boulevard, Hollywood; ///handwriting.chairs.payer; www.hollywoodsign.org

Ah, the Hollywood sign. Nothing symbolizes the alluring promise of Tinseltown quite like this fabled landmark. There are plenty of well-known places to see it from, including Griffith Observatory *(p176)* and the Ovation Hollywood shopping center. Our pick, though, is the top floor of the parking structure at the Home Depot on Sunset Boulevard – it's (sort of) like your own private viewing deck.

HOLLYWOOD WALK OF FAME

Map 3; Hollywood Boulevard, Hollywood; ///legs.friday.strict; walkoffame.com

There's no denying it's supremely touristy, but you can't really say you've been to L.A. without a stroll along this star-studded sidewalk. It's most fun if you make a game of it: look for obscure celebrities you forgot existed, and discover which unfortunate people have been consigned to the second-tier streets off Hollywood Boulevard. Bonus points if you can spot the two Harrison Fords – the one you (probably) haven't heard of was a silent film star.

» Don't leave without finding your celebrity hand and foot double among the prints outside Grauman's Chinese Theatre.

WARNER BROS STUDIO TOUR

Map 6; 3400 Warner Boulevard, Burbank; ///extra.counts.trips; www.wbstudiotour.com

Don't have any Hollywood connections? Then your best option for visiting a studio lot is to take the guided tour at Warner Bros. Yes, you could do something similar at Universal Studios or Disneyland, but only here can you see the actual *Friends* fountain (and the Central Perk café), as well as the apartment sets from *The Big Bang Theory*. Oh, and did we mention there's also a Batmobile you can look inside? If you're super lucky, you might even spot some celebrities filming (it does happen, we promise you).

Try it!
PRETTY WOMAN

Have your own Julia Roberts moment by going (window) shopping on Rodeo Drive. If you've got the budget, you can even book a full "Pretty Woman for a Day" experience at the Beverly Wilshire hotel from the movie.

Scenic Road Trips

When the weekend finally arrives, Angelenos have one thing in mind: a road trip. Make like a local and hit the road in search of California's most gorgeous spots and landscapes.

MULHOLLAND DRIVE

Map 3; start at Cahuenga Boulevard, Hollywood Hills; ///jaws.yarn.wire

Stuck in inner-city traffic? Fantasizing about a nonstop drive through the Hollywood Hills? Look no further than Mulholland Drive, a road so famous that David Lynch named a movie after it. The 21-mile (34-km) stretch runs east–west along the upper ridge of the mountains that separate the San Fernando Valley from L.A. proper. Aside from a glorious lack of traffic jams, you'll be rewarded with stunning vistas with every hairpin curve. Just take it slow, yeah?

OCEAN BOULEVARD

Map 5; start at Alamitos Beach, Long Beach; ///ruins.gives.pillows

At the southernmost end of L.A., on the Long Beach coast, the bike path parallel to Ocean Boulevard makes for an idyllic afternoon cycle. Channel your inner movie star by donning your sunglasses and pedal past the oceanfront condos and swaying palm trees that line

If you prefer four wheels to two, hop in your ride and drive the route along actual Ocean Boulevard.

this short, scenic route (it's just a few miles long). Continue east to Alamitos Park with extreme ocean views of sailboats, barges, and tropical-looking artificial islands.

PACIFIC COAST HIGHWAY

Map 6; start on Pacific Coast Highway, Santa Monica; ///guess.groom.plates

Picture a typical California road and you'll likely think of the Pacific Coast Highway, which traces the state's stunning coastline for 655 miles (1,005 km). Starting in L.A. as a series of urban boulevards, the highway is especially popular (read: busy) between Santa Monica and Malibu. And it's easy to see why: with mountains on one side and the Pacific Ocean on the other, cyclists and convertibles all slow to savor the salty air and ogle the beachfront mansions.

» **Don't leave without** taking your bike and enjoying a detour just north of the Santa Monica Pier to Venice Beach. The views are epic.

PALOS VERDES DRIVE SOUTH

Map 5; start at Western Avenue and 25th Street, San Pedro; ///rounded.inspections.employer

Ah, the heavenly Palos Verdes Peninsula: rugged Californian cliffs, deep-blue surf, and ocean-view houses atop it all. The scenery is constantly changing, too, thanks to the battering wind and waves eroding the dramatic landscape. Line up a playlist ("California Dreamin'," anyone?) and join the road from San Pedro for unparalleled views of the Pacific, Catalina Island, and untouched beaches below.

PALMS TO PINES SCENIC BYWAY

Map 6; start on Highway 74, Palm Desert; ///toddler.probing.suspect

Families climb into their SUVs, picnics in tow, and leave the city for this truly unique scenic byway. The 67-mile (108-km) road transforms from a desert oasis (near Coachella Valley, no less) into snow-peaked mountains, providing ample landscapes to stop for a stretch of the legs and an alfresco lunch.

HIGHWAY 101

Map 6; start at Los Angeles Street entrance to Highway 101, Downtown; ///slides.lower.belly

Highway 101 connects downtown L.A. with San Francisco, but locals know they don't have to travel all the way to the Bay to get dreamy coastal views. About an hour outside of L.A., mountains spring up on the right, and sand and sea glitters on the left. A few small towns of hardy seaside homes later and Santa Barbara appears, with its stroll-worthy pier, historical Spanish mission, and lively downtown: just the ticket for a warm Saturday afternoon.

» **Don't leave without** spending some time in Santa Barbara's "Funk Zone," an artistic neighborhood full of independent stores.

ANGELES CREST HIGHWAY

Map 6; start on Highway 2, La Cañada-Flintridge; ///fast.stands.then

Of course L.A. locals love their city, but sometimes a change of scene is needed. Thankfully, the Angeles Crest Highway is on hand to sweep weary office workers and creatively blocked artists out into the wilderness. For 66 miles (106 km), the scenic byway twists and winds around picturesque peaks, hugging the rim of the San Gabriel Mountains as they blend into the San Bernardino range and snaking around the iconic Mount Wilson Observatory.

JOSHUA TREE NATIONAL PARK

Map 6; start on Interstate 10, Santa Monica; ///shuts.spike.kick

Americans are rightly proud of their national parks – their shared backyards – which span every kind of landscape imaginable. Angelenos' closest park is Joshua Tree, famed for its otherworldly yucca palms. We say "close"; it's a good 127-mile (205-km) drive from L.A., making this the perfect summer road trip with friends (hello, car pool). Once your pals have piled into the car, take the Interstate 10 east through the windy fields of giant turbines, and up onto Highway 62. Stay on the 62 until you reach the park entrance in the city of Joshua Tree. Here, you'll be greeted by incredible views of the Mojave and Sonoran deserts and, importantly, a number of restaurants for a hard-earned meal.

Try it!
STARGAZING

After concentrating on the road to get to Joshua Tree, look up to the night sky. Park up at one of the park's roadside pullouts or camp and sleep beneath the stars *(home.nps.gov/jotr/index.htm)*.

VISTA DEL MAR

EL SEGUNDO

SAN DIEGO FREEWAY

1

Pick up your wheels at
MANHATTAN BEACH E-BIKE RENTALS

E-bikes are all the rage in L.A. Hire yours for the day at this dedicated rental hub and get pedaling.

ROSECRANS

MANHATTAN BEACH

2

Continue on to
BRUCE'S BEACH

Pause at the site of the West Coast's first Black-owned beach resort, which is now a hilltop park with views of the Strand below.

3

Fuel up at
MANHATTAN BEACH PIER

Stop for lunch in the South Bay's ultimate food area. Gastropub near the pier? Casual seafood by the ocean? You're spoiled for choice.

SOUTH BAY BIKE PATH

MANHATTAN BEACH

ARTESIA

Santa Monica Bay

HERMOSA BEACH

PACIFIC COAST HIGHWAY

4

Park up at
HERMOSA BEACH

Stop at Hermosa Beach for a refreshment and feel the punk history course through you: bands like Black Flag and Circle Jerks got their start at the bars here.

WEST 190T

South Bay *beaches are key to the U.S. surf scene – like Manhattan and Redondo, both name-checked in the Beach Boys'* "Surfin' U.S.A."

5

Kick back at
REDONDO BEACH PIER

Cruise along the International Boardwalk to the pier before chilling out with a craft beer. You've earned it.

0 kilometers 1

0 miles 1

REDONDO BEACH

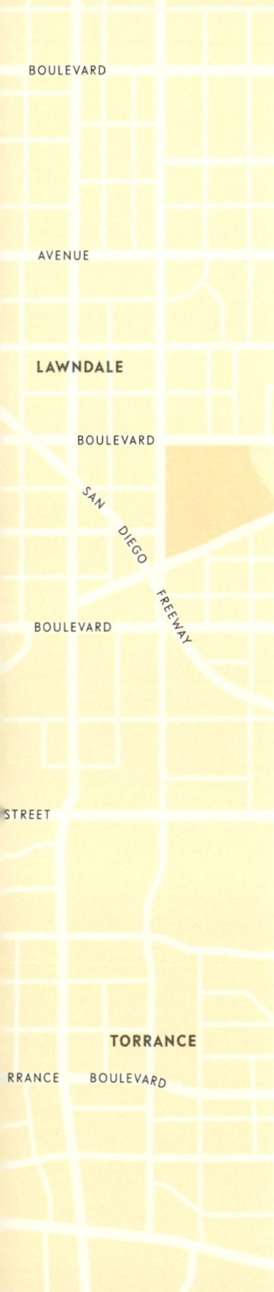

An afternoon cycling along the Strand

Sandy beaches, swaying palm trees, and a refreshing ocean breeze: L.A.'s coastline really does make for an idyllic cycle. And, thanks to a paved path known as the Strand, cyclists have 22 miles (35 km) of picturesque beachfront to pedal along. Our tip? Forget the stretch of the Strand that snakes alongside Santa Monica and Venice beaches, which are often overrun with tourists. Instead, start at Manhattan Beach, where a 5-mile (8-km) section is much less crowded and perfectly encapsulates L.A.'s coastal culture. And, yes, a postpedal drink is a must.

1. Manhattan Beach E-Bike Rentals
3616 Highland Avenue, Manhattan Beach; www.beachsidemb.com
///going.deals.pardon

2. Bruce's Beach
2600 Highland Avenue, Manhattan Beach
///wakes.normal.amuse

3. Manhattan Beach Pier
2 Manhattan Beach Boulevard
///clash.deeply.copies

4. Hermosa Beach
1 Pier Avenue
///hooked.prove.bikes

5. Redondo Beach Pier
Fisherman's Wharf, Redondo Beach
///achieving.oils.spin

With a little research and preparation, this city will feel like a home away from home. Check out these websites to ensure a healthy, safe stay in Los Angeles.

Los Angeles

DIRECTORY

SAFE SPACES

Los Angeles is a wonderfully diverse and largely progressive city, but should you feel uneasy or want to find your community at any point, there are spaces and resources to help you out.

www.discoverlosangeles.com/visit/the-guide-to-black-owned-businesses-in-la
Find Black-owned businesses across L.A.

www.elawc.org
Center offering social and advocacy services for women, with an emphasis on Latinx communities.

www.lacatholics.org/interreligious-resources
A list of local, national, and global interfaith resources compiled by L.A. Catholics.

www.lalgbtcenter.org
Nonprofit organization offering support for L.A.'s LGBTQ+ community.

HEALTH

Health care in the U.S. isn't free, so it's important to take out comprehensive health insurance for your visit. If you do need medical assistance, there are many pharmacies and hospitals across Los Angeles.

www.cvs.com/store-locator/cvs-pharmacy-locations/24-hour-pharmacies/California/Los-Angeles
Store locator showing 24-hour CVS pharmacies in the city.

www.dhs.lacounty.gov
The official website for L.A. county's Department of Health Services lists the area's hospitals and health centers.

www.outofthecloset.org/testing
This thrift store chain, which supports the AIDS Healthcare Foundation, runs a free HIV testing program.

www.plannedparenthood.org
National nonprofit organization providing sexual health care for all.

TRAVEL SAFETY INFORMATION

Before you travel – and while you're here – check the latest advice on how to stay safe in L.A. and the U.S.

www.fire.ca.gov/incidents
Regularly updated map of wildfire incidents in L.A., managed by the Department of Forestry and Fire Protection.

www.flylax.com/travelsafely
Los Angeles International Airport's official travel safety guide.

www.lapdonline.org/crime-prevention
Safety tips and information on how to report various crimes.

www.lapublichealth.org
The L.A. County Department of Public Health advises on disease prevention.

www.parks.ca.gov
Official site for California's state parks, with information on safety.

www.travel.state.gov
Latest travel safety information from the U.S. government.

ACCESSIBILITY

L.A. is often hailed as one of the best cities in the U.S. when it comes to accessibility. Most public transportation, hotels, and attractions are available to all people, but it's always best to check ahead.

www.acb.org
National organization providing resources and support to blind and partially sighted people.

www.brailleinstitute.org/losangeles
The Braille Institute Los Angeles' center runs workshops, seminars, and events.

www.dcrc.co
Designed and operated by people with disabilities, the Disability Community Resource Center provides resources, training, and support for the community.

https://disability.lacity.org
The official website for the City of Los Angeles' Department on Disability.

INDEX

ABOUT THE ILLUSTRATOR

Meet the illustrator

Award-winning British illustrator David Doran is based in a studio by the sea in Falmouth, Cornwall. When not drawing and designing, David tries to make the most of the beautiful area in which he's based: sea-swimming all year round, running the coastal paths and generally spending as much time outside as possible.

With thanks

DK would like to thank the following people for their contribution to the first edition of this book: Sarah Bennett, Ryan Gajewski, Anita Little, Eva Recinos, Elspeth Beidas, Lucy Richards, Tania Gomes and Casper Morris.

THIS EDITION UPDATED BY
Contributor Jess Esa
Project Editor Lucy Sara-Kelly
Senior Editor Zoë Rutland
Senior Designer Stuti Tiwari Bhatia
Cartography Manager Suresh Kumar
Cartographer Ashif
Jacket Designer Laura O'Brien
Jacket Illustrator David Doran
Senior DTP Designer Tanveer Zaidi
Production Controller Samantha Cross
Senior Managing Art Editor Priyanka Thakur
Editorial Director Hollie Teague
Art Director Maxine Pedliham
Publishing Director Georgina Dee

This book was made with Forest Stewardship Council™ certified paper – one small step in DK's commitment to a sustainable future.
Learn more at **www.dk.com/uk/information/sustainability**

A NOTE FROM DK

The world is fast-changing and it's keeping us folk at DK on our toes. We've worked hard to ensure that this edition of Los Angeles Like a Local is up-to-date and reflects today's favourite places but we know that standards shift, venues close and new ones pop up in their place. So, if you notice something has closed, we've got something wrong or left something out, we want to hear about it. Drop us a line at travelguides@dk.com

First edition 2022

Published in Great Britain by Dorling Kindersley Limited, 20 Vauxhall Bridge Road, London SW1V 2SA

The authorised representative in the EEA is Dorling Kindersley Verlag GmbH. Arnulfstr. 124, 80636 Munich, Germany

Published in the United States by DK Publishing, 1745 Broadway, 20th Floor, New York, NY 10019, USA

24 25 26 27 10 9 8 7 6 5 4 3 2 1

A CIP catalog record for this book is available from the British Library.

A catalog record for this book is available from the Library of Congress.

ISSN: 1542 1554
ISBN: 9780 2417 2969 4

Printed and bound in China.

www.dk.com